THE FATHER
AND
HIS FAMILY

A RESTATEMENT
of the
PLAN OF REDEMPTION

By

E. W. KENYON

Nineteenth Edition

PRINTED IN U. S. A.

E. W. KENYON, Author

1857 - 1948

Index

I. THE REASON FOR CREATION 19

II. MAN'S TREASON 29

III. THE DOMINION OF DEATH 45

IV. SATAN 57

V. HELL 73

VI. MAN'S NEED OF A MEDIATOR 85

VII. THE HUMANITY AND DEITY OF JESUS 97

VIII. HOW GOD CAN BE JUST 109

IX. THE SIN BEARER 121

X. ETERNAL LIFE 141

XI. THE NEW BIRTH 147

XII. THE HOLY SPIRIT 163

XIII. THE NEW LAW OF THE FAMILY 171

XIV. THE HOUSEHOLD OF GOD 181

XV. CLAIMING OUR RIGHTS 191

XVI. GOD WANTS TRANSFIGURED BODIES 205

XVII. MORTALITY AND IMMORTALITY 211

XVIII. RIGHTEOUSNESS 219

XIX. FELLOWSHIP 225

XX. HOW TO BECOME A CHRISTIAN 229

First Words

Thinking men and women of this age have been rebelling against the orthodox interpretation of the Bible as presented in denominational creeds.

A spirit of unrest has seized the heart of Christendom; many of the old landmarks of Faith have been destroyed by modern Criticism.

The Faith of millions has been shattered; the Church has lost its grip on the imagination of the age; the ministry is wandering in the byways of unbelief; they have found an interrogation point on every signboard of theological thought.

There is almost no coherence of doctrine in any of our great denominational bodies.

We are confronted with questions which demand answers.

Here is the world, a universe, a human family; why are they?

Science has not answered the question nor attempted to solve the problem.

We came to believe in the early days of our investigation that there could be no enduring system of Science, Philosophy, or Theology that was not based upon an intelligent answer to the age-long problem of the "Why of Creation."

I believe that the answer to these questions will be found in the following pages.

I believe that the Faith of those who read will be strengthened, that knowledge will take the place of vague speculations, and strength, the place of weakness.

The Father Fact

The Father Fact and the Family Fact are the two mightiest facts of the Bible; the Plan of Redemption swings about this two-fold center.

These two basic facts of revelation have been covered by the verbiage of Theological speculation.

The whole Plan of Redemption is:

First, the Father God's Dream for a Family.

Second, Redemption from a Sin Catastrophe.

Third, the Dream Coming True.

Fourth, the Family Home, the New Heavens and the New Earth.

The entire Plan of Redemption is a revelation of the heart-hunger and loneliness of the great Father God; the first step in this stupen. dous drama of Creation was God's dream and His blueprints of Man's beautiful Home.

No prospective husband-father ever dreamed more ardently of the home-nest than did the Father God dream over the contemplated home of His child — the human: so He took ages on ages to build an earth-home, to store it with treasures that only His mind could conceive and His power create.

After He had perfected an earth, He placed the stars and suns and moons and wonderful constellations throughout space, and to each of these seen as well as unseen worlds He fastened the earth by the invisible cords of gravitation.

Each star and constellation is held in its place by the word of His power, and each one has a regular course marked out over which it travels.

Each star and planet, each constellation and group has its own office work to perform for the earth, God's wonderful home for His human, His child, His family.

This book is a story of Love's processes to save man from himself and to present him a faultless, happy family in the presence of the living Father God.

The Family Fact

Christianity is not a religion; it is a family, a Father and His children.

It differs from all the religions in the world in this respect.

It is not a creed, nor a set of Doctrines, nor a body of Ethics.

Creeds have been made out of it.

Laws have been made out of it.

Doctrines have been formulated from its teachings, and the world's best Ethics have been its products.

They are all parts of it, segments of the great Family Fact.

The genius of Christianity is that its God is the great Family God of the Universe.

Christianity is not a science any more than your family is a Science, but it is based upon scientific facts.

Christianity is not a Philosophy, but it is the Revelation of the divine-human relationships.

Christianity is not a Theology, it is the reality of man's Redemption and union with God.

Author's Preface

THE TWO KINDS OF KNOWLEDGE

Years ago in California, a miner found his claim was giving out. He had built a cabin. It had become a home to him. His heart was utterly discouraged. Prospect after prospect had failed him.

Sitting in front of the cabin one morning he decided to plant some flowers. Taking his pick and shovel he began to work. He had worked but a few moments when he uncovered one of the richest veins of ore in that entire section.

He had walked over it for years.

The same thing is true in regard to one of the most remarkable discoveries we have ever made in the Word.

The difference between the miner and ourselves is this: we have known this fact in a vague way, but never realized its significance.

We did not know that it solved the whole rationalistic attitude of the scholastic world toward the Bible.

We did not know that it solved the problem of Biblical interpretation.

We did not know that it was the solution for the condition of the modern church.

We did not know that it solved the problem of the apostasy of a large part of our theological schools.

It is the amazing fact that there are two Kinds of Knowledge in the world today, and we have never contrasted them or compared them.

One is the Knowledge that we teach in our great universities, technical schools, and colleges.

The other is Knowledge that comes from the book called the Bible.

One is Knowledge that we have obtained through the Five Senses; the other is a Revelation from God.

It is an acknowledged fact that all the knowledge that the Scientific world, the Educational world and the Mechanical world have today has come through these Five Senses of Seeing, Hearing, Feeling, Tasting and Smelling.

Every contact that man has ever had with the universe has come to him through his Five Senses. He has gained no knowledge independently of them.

We may illustrate the limitation of sense knowledge by the following example: A blind man who has never possessed the sense of sight, could never know anything of color; a deaf man who had never heard, could never know anything of sound.

So we also with our Five Senses know nothing except as it has come to our minds through these five channels.

In other words that vast body of knowledge has come through experimentation.

Our bodies have been the source of this knowledge.

We call it Sense Knowledge.

It comes through Sense Perception. Our bodies have really been experimenting stations.

The vast knowledge of Chemistry, Metallurgy, and Mechanics has come through man's persistent experiments.

It is no wonder that these men who have only contacted the physical through their Sense Perceptions should deny the existence of God, because they cannot find Him in the material world.

They cannot find spirit nor soul through their experiments in Chemistry or Biology.

You can see why they naturally would rule out the supernatural, why miracles would be impossible to them.

They do not realize the fact that there are just as great realities in the realm of the spirit as in the realm of the material.

They have failed to grasp the fact that man is a spirit being, and that a Revelation from God was imperative.

This Revelation Knowledge leads us into the realm of miracles.

By this Revelation we have come to know God as a real Father.

We have been able to contact Him, able to bring Him into the material world where we have come to know Him.

Sense Knowledge cannot know God, cannot find Him, cannot see Him, hear Him nor feel Him.

Consequently in their realm they deny His existence.

You can understand now why a man who has never been Born Again cannot expound the Scriptures and give us their spiritual content.

Only a man whose mind has been illuminated by the New Birth can know God or understand His Revelation.

This explains why the church should not have taken so seriously the criticisms of the Bible by men of great scholarship who had never been Born Again.

Some of these men have even translated the Bible. We do not question their honesty or their scholarship. They did the best that a man with mere Sense Knowledge could do. We would not feel like criticizing a blind man for his attempt to interpret one of our great masterpieces of art.

This explains why Dr. Darwin gave to us the Darwinian Hypothesis of Evolution.

Sense Knowledge is limited. Natural man does not know the source of life, the source of matter, the origin of man, or the origin of the animal kingdom.

He knows nothing of how creation came into being.

He feels that he must give some explanation, and so he guesses.

Evolution is largely made up of guesses.

We have God's declaration of how all these came into being.

Sense Knowledge repudiates it, and we can understand that.

It would be unnatural for them to do otherwise.

We can see now the limitations of Sense Knowledge. It is explained fully in 1 Cor. 2: and is climaxed in this: (14th verse) "Now the natural man receiveth not the things of the Spirit of God: for they are foolishness unto him; and he cannot know them, because they are spiritually understood."

We are told here that the natural man cannot know the things of God, because they are spiritually discerned. He can only know material things.

We can understand this, for we know that every contact that man has with the outward world is through his central nervous system and its five senses, (the sense of sight, hearing, touch, taste, and smell).

These senses belong to the physical body, and they can only contact matter.

Therefore, man knows only that which is physically discerned. He has learned a great deal about the universe in which he lives but nothing about the Creator. As Voltaire has said, he has been able to study the stars but himself he has not come to know.

God has met man on his own level and given to him a revelation that he can contact with his five senses.

1 Cor. 2:12, 13 tells us how He has done it: "Now we have received not the spirit which is of the world but the spirit which is from God that we might know the things that are freely given to us of God. Which things we speak, not in words which man's wisdom teacheth, but which the spirit teacheth combining spiritual things with spiritual words."

This shows us that in words which man can see with his sense of sight and hear with his sense of hearing God has given a revelation of His plans and purposes to man.

The question might arise in the minds of some: Why is it that God created man in such a way that it would be impossible for him to know Him without a revelation?

God created man, as we shall see more fully in a later chapter of this book, a spirit being and gave to him a body for the home of the spirit. Through his physical body man was to contact the outward world which was to be his home. This knowledge of this world was to come to him through the medium of his five senses. The purpose of the nervous system was never to reveal God to man; man was to know God through his spirit.

When man died spiritually, that is, became alienated from God, he was left without a channel through which he could know God. It then became necessary for God to meet man on the level of the medium through which he gained his knowledge.

God has done this and this revelation is known to us as the Bible.

The natural man, the physical man, the man with only Sense Knowledge cannot understand this Revelation of God.

He must be re-created, his mind illuminated before he can judge spiritual things.

So the church need not be terrified by the new atheistic attitude toward the Bible.

Practically all the modern scientists show in their writings a hunger for God, but they cannot find Him with Sense Knowledge.

We have written this book to show the Sense Knowledge people the need of a Revelation, and the facts that are revealed in this Revelation.

"The more profoundly phenomena have been studied by scientists and scientific philosophers the more gloriously have shown out the truths to which I have alluded: that God has busied Himself through untold ages in preparing for man's advent, that man has been the grand goal of His endeavor, the ultimate Thule of His creative thought on this planet; that all this prolonged preparation could not have been merely to render comfortable a short-lived and low-planed animal existence; that this patient approach could not have been to a consummation so inconsequential and unworthy, but that he for whom the centuries have been so long waiting and wears the crown surely was not born to die."—
W. W. KINSLEY.

Chapter The First

THE REASON FOR CREATION

REATION SHOWS the Designer's Master Hand. Blind Chance is not its author.

Whether you explore the mysteries of the mineral kingdom, the vegetable or the animal, from the lowest to the highest, the marks of a well thought-out design confront you everywhere.

Nothing has been left to Chance.

Creation has been governed with the iron hand of fixed laws.

The microscope reveals this even among the most minute forms of life.

That same law prevails from the lowest germ cell to the highest forms of Creation.

An intelligent purpose pervades it all.

There is a grand focal objective in every step of Creation.

He who laid the foundation of the earth had the same plan and purpose, the same blueprints as He who put the last finishing touches upon it.

It may seem strange; nevertheless it is true, that Science has given no adequate reason for Creation.

She has been silent here, and yet this is where she should have launched her first ship of exploration.

There can be no scheme of Cosmogony that does not explain the "Why of Creation."

If Creation is a child of blind, unreasoning, undesigning Chance, Chance is a miracle worker and worthy of our adoration.

Philosophy that recognizes no Holy of Holies in any department of human endeavor has not attempted to answer this question and has left no footprints in these halls; her voice has never been heard in this debate.

The poet alone has turned his lyre to this lofty theme.

Theology, the Mother of the Sciences and Arts and the Inspiration of all Philosophies, has never yet given a reason for Creation.

She has built a mighty superstructure without a foundation; she has argued fluently of Divine Sovereignty and Freedom of Will, but she has been mute here.

Her theologians have found more pleasure in abstract Theology than in personal dealings with God, found more joy in Metaphysics than in divine knowledge, more pleasure in the opinions of men than in the Word of God.

Neither Science, Philosophy nor Theology has ever yet been able to write a textbook that would survive a generation.

We have forgotten that Truth is Eternal, while Theories are time limited.

No one thinks of revising the multiplication table.

Truth has never needed a revision. Theories are revised from age to age.

In spite of all the assaults and ridicule that have been hurled at the first three Chapters of Genesis, they still stand as the only intelligent mind-satisfying reason for Creation. It may be interesting for us to notice first that that portion of Scripture declares that the Earth is the reason for all heavenly bodies that swing in their mighty orbits through dark, illimitable space.

GENESIS HISTORY

Genesis compels a complete reconstruction of our Theories of Creation.

Genesis 1:14-19, "And God said, Let there be lights in the firmament of heaven to divide the day from the night; and let them be for signs, and for seasons, and for days and years: and let them be for lights in the firmament of heaven to give light upon the earth: and it was so.

"And God made the two great lights; the greater light to rule the day, and the lesser light to rule the night: he made the stars also.

"And God set them in the firmament of heaven to give light upon the earth and to rule over the day and over the night, and to divide the light from the darkness and God saw that it was good.

"And there was evening and there was morning a fourth day."

You will notice in this statement that the Earth was already created and held in its place by the Word of God.

Now He begins to place suns, moons, stars, and planets in their respective positions in the firmament to minister to this Earth, to divide the days and nights, to give us signs and seasons, days and years.

It would seem from this Scripture that the Earth is the reason for the Universe.

As far as we know from the best Astronomers, our Earth is the only planet in the Universe that has life upon it.

If this be true, it proves that the Earth holds a place in the plan and purpose of God that is amazing.

To refer once more to our quotation from Scripture, "to let them be for signs and for seasons, and for days and years and to give light upon the Earth."

We know that the tides of the oceans and seas are affected by the influence of the heavenly bodies.

We know that heat and cold, drought and storm are the direct results of planetary influence.

We know that storms can be predicted for certain localities on this continent by the position and influence of certain planets.

This is being done from week to week; it has become one of the assured Sciences.

An earthquake can be predicted years ahead, because certain planets will focalize their influence for an hour upon a certain point of the Earth's surface which will cause a convulsion.

We know that frosts and heat waves are predicted months ahead by the sure knowledge of planetary positions.

From these deductions we see clearly that the planets were placed in the heavens to give us seasons, to be signs, to be the continual companions and servants, always ministering to the Earth.

Once more we want to state that this proves that the Earth is the reason for that great star spangled universe we call the heavens.

To illustrate this it might be interesting to relate a story that is being told of a noted astronomer who was discussing with his son one day the influence of the heavenly bodies on the Earth.

He made this remark, "I have noticed that at certain times the Earth is lifted out of her orbit or path by an unseen body lying beyond the reach of our most powerful telescope. If ever they build a larger telescope, I wish you would go and search the heavens to find out what it is that so affects this planet of ours."

When the great Lick Observatory was reared with its powerful telescope this son traveled across sea and continent, and one clear night turned the great telescope against the dark space in the heavens where this unseen, uncharted planet reached down its mighty hand and gripped the Earth.

After gazing awhile, suddenly there appeared a tiny speck of light; it was a star swinging in its giant orbit away out on the frontier of the Universe.

He saw the planet that had so strangely affected the earth. It was millions of miles beyond the farthest star that the human eye had ever seen.

Yet, this giant star sweeping on its great orbit came regularly every few years close enough to our planet, so that it could reach its mighty hand of gravitation down through the unmeasured space and grip our little earth and lift it out of its orbit.

As a ship on the ocean responds to the slightest touch of the helm, our Earth responds to the touch of that distant sentinel and veers swiftly out of its course; then when the planet's grip is loosed, back into its path it comes and goes rhythmically on its way.

This establishes one fact: that there is neither planet, nor sun, nor moon, nor star in all the vast universe but has its influence upon this little planet of ours.

How it thrills the heart to realize that this Earth of ours, so small that one thousand of them can be lost in the sun, is the center and reason for the Universe.

Tonight this old Earth of ours is being held as safely in the embrace of those uncounted and uncharted planets as a child in its mother's arms.

The heavens are tonight Earth's only perfect timepiece; no watch or clock ever built by man can give us perfect time; but he who knows the path of the stars knows that every star, or sun, or planet will pass a certain given point in the great unpathed space on schedule time.

The star may not have been seen for thousands of years, but she will appear at the cross-roads of the heavens not one second ahead nor one second behind her schedule.

Oh! the wonder of the Architect, the marvel of the Creator, the might of the Sustainer of this great universe of ours!

THE REASON FOR THE EARTH

If the Earth is the reason for the stellar heavens, what is the reason for the Earth?

Before the Morning Stars sang their first anthem to the heart of the lonely 'Father God, before the foundations of the Earth were laid, before the first rays of light ever passed through the dark expanse, the heart of the great Creator God had a yearning, deep, mighty, eternal.

It was the primordial passion for children.

The Father heart of the Creator God longed for sons and daughters.

This yearning passion took form, and God planned a universe for His Man, and in the heart of that universe He purposed a Home.

There is no time with God.

Time belongs to day and night, to sun and moon.

The Omnipotent God was not hampered by days, nor nights, nor years.

When Love laid the foundations of this mighty universe, He planned, He purposed it all to be the Home of His Man.

It was to be Man's birthplace, Man's Garden of Delight, Man's University where he would learn to know his Father God.

Love took plenty of time.

Ages and ages He worked storing up treasures of all kinds of wealth for His Man.

He filled Earth's bosom with deposits of iron, copper, silver, and gold, with uncounted varieties of metals, chemicals, and resources that would respond to the touch of His Man.

He covered the face of the Earth with mountains, valleys, ravines, plateaus, and prairies, lovely rivulets and mighty rivers, and a garment of green intermingled with many colored flowers that thrilled with joy the heart of His Man.

The mountain sides are covered with giant forests, whose trees are filled with singing birds and droning insects, whose dainty wings beat against the genial wind and make a melody fit for His Man.

Fruits and vegetables abound in profusion, spelling out in nature's language the love of the great Father heart of God for His Man.

This interprets the great dream, the heart plan, the great Father God has for His Man.

The Architect knew on what sections of the earth's surface the human would segregate, and there He placed His great deposits of copper, of iron ore, of coal, limestone, and all the other natural resources and chemicals necessary for the arts, mechanics, and the sciences.

Wherever there are vast prairies for grain support for the millions of earth's teeming population, near it you will find the greatest deposits of chemicals and metals, and minerals and oils.

He grouped them so that they would be ready for man's need. Chance did not rule here.

Had platinum and gold been as plentiful as iron, and iron as scarce as gold, there never would have been a mechanical age.

The steel rails that gird the earth, that bind nations together would have been impossible; the mighty Mogul engine could never have been built of gold or copper.

The great Architect of human need and joy knew man's need while yet unborn, and in Creation's wondrous plan these needs were met.

Animal Kingdom

In the animal creation it will be interesting to note that there are today approximately twenty-five domestic animals.

Scientists have tried to tell us that the dog and house cat were formerly wild and have simply been domesticated, but nature contradicts it.

There is a dog to meet every need of man from the Arctic to the equator and from the rising to the setting of the sun.

The strange thing about it is that no wild animals as yet have ever been able to take the place of our domestics.

They tell us that the dog belongs to the wolf family, but who has ever been able to take a wolf of any species and tame it to make a lap-dog of it, a guard and companion to his children, or a daily associate on the farm or home? You may keep him twenty generations, and he is still a wolf.

If you let our faithful friend of the human go wild in the forest for twenty generations, then capture and take him to your home, within a week he is your servant and friend and slave who will lay his life down for you.

The dog was created by God Almighty to be the faithful servant and companion and lover of man.

Our common house-cat was created to be the household friend and chum of children and childhood, and pet of the aged.

When the wise Master Builder made the horse He designed him purposely to meet the needs of His Man as servant and beast of burden.

He left a place in its mouth where no teeth grow that a bit might be held without inconvenience, that the horse might be able to eat its food with the bit still in its mouth.

Had the cow been given the fierce disposition of a hyena or lion, she would have been totally unfit for domestic purposes.

Had the dog been given the disposition of the wolf or fox, or had our cat been given the disposition of the tiger, they would have been unsafe for our home.

Had the horse been given the disposition of the zebra, it never would have been man's beast of burden and inseparable friend.

No, He who created man knew that man would need domestic animals that would respond to the touch of love, animals that would pine and yearn for human companionship and that would gladly obey the human voice. So I might speak of the other domestic animals that show the wise provision of an intelligent creator, if I had space.

VEGETABLE KINGDOM

It will be of intense interest for us to look at the great variety of woods that were created for Man.

There are 183 varieties of the Eucalyptus family alone. These with the oak, the sighing pine, the laughing maple, the delicate willow, the lonely poplar were created to fill a need and want in humanity's development and expansion.

There are over one hundred thousand classified varieties in the vegetable kingdom; there are over five hundred thousand insects that feed on these hundred thousand varieties.

Every plant, shrub, vegetable, fruit or tree of the entire vegetable kingdom was designed and planned for man's use, and as man grows intellectually and delves into the mysteries of the vegetable kingdom he is finding there the answer to thousands of needs that are continually coming in this great mechanical age.

The Reason For Man

If the Earth is the reason for the heavens, and Man is the reason for the Earth, what is the reason for Man?

There is only one answer, and it is very simple: the lonely heart of the great Father God.

Paul tells us in Ephesians that "all Fatherhood heads up in God, whether the families on earth or the families in heaven."

God's heart yearned for children, craved sons and daughters.

He had angels to minister to Him as servants, but He wanted children, so He spent with Love's wonderful patience age on age in the preparation of the Earth and Heavens for His Man.

If this be true, and true it is; then Man is a most wonderful Being.

If God so wanted Man and so loved Man that He spent millions of years in preparation for him, what a place that Man must hold in His heart, in His dream, in His Eternity!

Questions

1. How does Creation reveal a designer?
2. What scripture shows the earth to be the reason for the heavenly universe?
3. How does the earth with its treasures interpret God's dream and plan for the human?
4. How do the domestic animals reveal God's thoughtful provision for man's needs?
5. What is the reason for man?

"Man has become master of the world. Other creatures hold their lives at his pleasure; the earth yields her stores of fruits, fuels, and minerals to his machinery; he collects power from the rivers and the sun; he communicates his thoughts around the world almost instantaneously; he explores the universe with his telescope and spectroscope; and he rides on air, land, and water at speeds exceeding that of the swiftest of birds."

(Even in his fallen and dethroned estate man bears traces of his original position as master of the universe.)

Chapter The Second

MAN'S TREASON

IS the present condition of man normal?

Are we living under the Father's ideal and plan for the human?

Are sin, sickness, and death a part of God's plan? Is He their Author?

Are hatred, jealousy, and murder a part of God's plan?

Are the unnatural fratricidal wars that sweep the earth a part of God's original purpose?

Did God have an original plan without sin, without pain, without grief, without hate, and without death?

NATURE OF MAN

We believe that God's heart is the reason not only for creation, but for creation's crown, Man.

"Blessed be the God and Father of our Lord Jesus Christ, who hath blessed us with every spiritual blessing in the heavenly places in Christ: even as He chose us in Him before the foundation of the world, that we should be holy and without blemish before Him, in love having foreordained us unto adoption as sons through Jesus Christ unto Himself, according to the good pleasure of His will." Ephesians 1:3-5.

Man was marked out for sonship before the foundation of the world. Love marked us out for adoption as sons through Jesus Christ unto Himself.

In other words, before the foundation of the world He purposed a family, and Man is the answer to that purpose.

What kind of being was Man in the beginning?

In Genesis 1, it declares that Man was created in God's own image after His own likeness.

29

What is meant by "in His own image and likeness"?

From what we know of the original Man, God created him to be His companion and Eternal associate.

He is a spirit being, although he lives in a physical body.

Eccl. 3:11 — "God set eternity in his heart."

We know that he was created to be the companion of the Creator; he was not to fill the place of a servant to a Master or a domestic animal to its owner but was to be a son and fellow companion, an associate of the Eternal Father throughout Eternity.

It might be interesting before we go into the subject more fully to note the kind of a being Man was at the beginning.

Kind of Man

Darwin's hypothesis of evolution that grew out of Sense Knowledge has thrown her dark cloud of unbelief and fatalism over the age and makes Truth hard to be understood, but in the face of this we want to prosecute our investigation.

In our narrow limits it will be impossible for us to enter into the discussion of evolution.

It is sufficient to say that the latest dictum of Science is that there are three distinct kinds of Life and that these three are separated by impassable chasms; namely, Vegetable Life, Animal Life, and Human Life.

The Vegetable can never cross the chasm to the Animal, and the Animal can never cross over to the Human.

This forever destroys the Darwinian hypothesis, that was born in the realm of the senses.

We might call attention to the fact that in their wild state no animals even of the same species ever crossed; the different varieties never mingled.

Nowhere either in fossil or in forest fastness was there ever found a cross between the bear and the deer, the deer and the tiger, the lion and the hyena, or the crow and the robin, the hawk and the dove, or the horse and the elephant.

Genesis 1:24-25 — "And God said, let the earth bring forth living creatures after their kind, cattle, and creeping things, and beasts of the earth after their kind: and it was so. And God made the beasts of the earth after their kind, cattle after their kind, and everything that creepeth upon the earth after its kind: and God saw that it was good."

After a most careful and searching examination of fossils in all stages in animal history this statement of Genesis remains true, every animal "after its own kind."

The skeptic cannot find one place in all animal history where there was ever a cross of species from the most minute organism to the largest of mammals; everything has stayed in its own class by itself.

You can find the fern embedded in the great beds of coal, but it is the same fern that you picked today in the cool shade of the forest.

The maple leaf that is found embedded down eleven hundred feet underground, underneath the strata of coal is the same maple leaf that we know; there is no change in it; it has the same number of points, the same shape as the maple leaf that grows on your lawn.

The same form of life that we find today in the bed of the ocean is found in the rocks; it has never changed.

No, Nature knows her laws, and the wild animal lives in perfect obedience to them.

MAN, THE CROWN OF CREATION

Scriptures declare that when man was created he had a mind intellectually of such a character that he was able to name the entire animal creation.

"And out of the ground Jehovah God formed every beast of the field, and every bird of the heavens; and brought them to the Man to see what he would call them: and whatsoever the man called every living creature, that was the name thereof."

And the man gave names to all cattle, and all birds of the heavens, and to all beasts of the field, and the name that was given described the characteristics and nature of the animal.

When we realize that there are more than 500,000 bugs, birds, worms, animals, fish and reptiles, and that man named them, we realize that he could not have been any half developed missing link of the Simian family. No! he came full-orbed from the womb of Creation, fit to be ruler over creation.

He was not only created with an intellect of such marvelous powers but also with spiritual capacities that made him the fit companion of Deity.

MAN'S DOMINION

Again, God gave him dominion over all the works of His hands, as described in Gen. 1:28 and Psalm 8:3, 4.

"When I consider thy heavens, the work of Thy fingers, the moon and the stars, which Thou hast ordained; what is man that Thou art mindful of him? And the son of man, that Thou visited him?

"Thou has made him but little lower than the angels."
(The Hebrew word translated "angels" in this verse is the same word translated "God" in Genesis 1:1, and should have been translated as follows:

"Thou hast made him but little lower than God, and crowned him with glory and honor, and made him to have dominion over all the works of Thy hands, and put all things under his feet.")

Notice here that man is made but little lower than God.

As one eminent Hebraist translates: "Thou hast made him but a shade lower than God."

In other words, when man was created he was made as near like Deity as it was possible for Deity to create him.

He was made to be God's companion.

Next you notice that God gave him dominion over all the works of His hands.

He ruled not only the animal creation but he also ruled the laws of Creation.

He ruled the very stars in their courses.

He was God's under-ruler.

He was the subject of no being or law save God and the Law of Love.

This in itself is a most remarkable fact, but it perfectly coincides with man's dreams of dominion.

Man was never made to be a subject or slave.

We see glimpses of man's dominion down through the ages of humanity's history.

Moses had the dominion over the Laws of Nature when he spoke to the Red Sea. It opened before him, a huge gap cut by an unseen hand, with its walls towering hundreds of feet on either side; there it stood at the voice of a man, till four million people with their stock and herds, their families and slaves, went pouring through dry-shod to liberty on the other side; and then by the same voice of that same man the waters came thundering together with a crash that shook the heathen nations for generations.

We see Joshua speaking to the Jordan, and that turbulent river responded to the voice of its master and opened a path for triumphant Israel to reach its promised land. We hear the same man speaking to the sun and moon, and they stood still hour after hour while he wrought a victory over his enemies.

We see the intrepid Elijah calling fire out of heaven.

We see Daniel's three companions thrown into the fiery furnace and come out without a burn or smell of fire on their garments.

Then we quietly drop down through the ages to the Nazarene and see Him exercising the same authority given to man at the beginning.

Jesus, having been born free from the taint of Mortality, held the same Authority and Dominion as the first man.

We see Jesus exercising this Authority over the Sea of Galilee, over the maimed legs and arms of suffering humanity, over death, and over the fish of the sea, over the trees of the field, and over Satan.

Jesus ruled as absolute Master and Monarch of Creation.

Man's Nature

When Man was created, he was planned a perfect human being with endless human life.

He was neither Immortal nor Mortal.

The word mortal means "death-doomed" or "Satan-ruled."

Immortality means freedom from the dominion of mortality, incorruptible, deathless.

When God created Adam he was a perfect human being; death had no dominion over him.

He had physical life that had the power of recuperation to the extent that he never wore out; nor was he subject to disease or death.

I suppose that the Physiological Law that man's physical nature renews itself once in seven years was the secret of man's perennial freshness physically.

Jesus had the same kind of a physical body. He was not subject to death. Death had no authority over Him until He became our sin-substitute and our sin-nature was laid upon Him; then He became Mortal and subject to Death.

Man belongs to God's class.

He is an eternal personality.

Before he committed sin, he had Dominion over all angels and demons.

No being but God Almighty, Himself, was greater.

It might be well for us to notice at this point another remarkable feature in God's plan.

TIME LIMIT

God gave to man a Time-Limit Dominion; by accommodation we might call it a Lease of Dominion.

This Lease of Dominion is called in Daniel and in Mark, "the age of the Gentiles," that is, the age of the nations, or the age of the Dominion of Man.

"And behold, they cried out, saying, What have we to do with Thee, Thou Son of God? art Thou come hither to torment us before the time?" Matt. 8:29.

"And Jerusalem shall be trodden down of the Gentiles, until the times of the Gentiles be fulfilled." Luke 21:24.

The word "Gentiles" means the "Human Race," fallen man.

"For I would not, brethren, have you ignorant, of this mystery, lest ye be wise in your own conceits, that a hardening in part hath befallen Israel until the fulness of the Gentiles be come in." Romans 11:25.

"Therefore rejoice, O heavens, and ye that dwell in them. Woe for the earth and for the sea: because the devil is gone down unto you, having great wrath, knowing that he hath but a short time." Rev. 12:12.

In these Scriptures we see that the demons knew they had a Time-limit.

That Time-limit is called the Time of the Gentiles.

This evidently means the Age of Man's original Dominion which was turned over to Satan.

We know that Satan is ruling today through fallen man, but, thank God, that Lease is nearly ended and will expire at the Coming of the Lord Jesus.

MAN'S RESPONSIBILITY

God gave to man the ability to reproduce himself, to beget children.

It happened in this wise.

God, instead of creating the whole human race by a single word, created one man and one woman, and said to them, "I permit you to give birth to My children, to rear, educate, and care for them, teaching them to love Me and respond to My heart yearnings."

So, man's real business was to give birth to God's children.

This gives a responsibility to man that can only be measured by Eternity.

Man gives birth to eternal personalities, children who will live as long as God lives.

Man is then the Custodian of God's joy.

NATURE OF MAN'S SIN

This is the old problem that has confronted Theologians in every generation since Calvary.

What was the nature of man's original transgression?

It could not have been a broken law for there had been no law given as we understood the term from its connection with the Law of Moses.

Then what kind of a sin was it that could compel the Incarnation and the sufferings of Calvary?

What was the sin that may be called man's masterstroke of misery?

Having found that man was invested with such far-reaching authority, that he had an intellect of such calibre as to be the companion of Deity, and that he had in his hands the joy or the sorrow of God, we can understand now the nature of the sin he committed.

High Treason

The sin of Adam was the crime of High Treason.

God had conferred upon him the legal authority to rule the Universe.

This Universe-wide Dominion was the most sacred heritage that God could give to Man.

Adam turned this Legal Dominion into the hands of God's enemy, the Devil.

This sin is unpardonable! High Treason has been so considered in all ages of the Human.

Adam's transgression was committed in the white light of absolute knowledge.

He was not deceived by the Devil.

He understood the steps that led to this awful crime.

His wife, Eve, was deceived, but Adam became the Benedict Arnold of Eternity. "For Adam was first formed, then Eve; and Adam was not beguiled, but the woman being beguiled hath fallen into transgression." I Timothy 2:13-14.

He knew God; he knew Satan; he knew the result of the unthinkable crime he committed.

The Effect of the Treason

First, it was the thwarting of God's plan.

Second, it was the separation of God and Man.

Third, it gave Satan universal Dominion over God's creation.

Fourth, it incurred a complete bondage of the Human to the Devil.

Fifth, it brought a blighting Curse upon the Animal and the Vegetable Kingdom.

There had been no death since the face of the earth had been renewed and prepared for man's advent, but now a blighting curse sweeps over God's fair Creation.

Every flower and fruit has a curse upon it.

Worms, briars and thorns abound.

In Genesis 3:17 the story is told of the earth's being cursed as a result of man's sin.

So bitterly was it cursed that its fruit was unfit to lay upon God's altar as we see in Cain's offering.

This hideous, withering curse changed the face of all the earth.

Death and blight are now visible everywhere.

The effect on the animal kingdom is more striking.

Creation was planned under the dominion of love; the whole animal creation lived in the atmosphere of love and peace.

Fear and hatred were unknown.

Suddenly the whole animal creation received a new nature.

There was breathed into them as by a breath of wind a spirit of hatred, of cunning, of fear, and revenge.

The lamb and lion had gamboled and played together upon the green; suddenly the lion is changed; he becomes ferocious; his voice that had known no sounds but love was changed until the very woods and plains resounded with his awful war-call.

Fear grips the heart of the timid.

Man's awful crime is being felt by the whole animal creation.

The earth is suddenly turned into a great battlefield, and down through the ages the silent woods, streams, and deserts have become a huge cemetery.

Fear and death stalk in the shadows of every night.

Man's Kingdom

Man suddenly becomes mortal.

Man becomes death-doomed, Satan's servant.

He is born again.

He is more than a sinner; he is sin.

A new Nature enters into him.

It is not the nature of God but of this enemy, the Devil. A similar nature is breathed into the Animal Kingdom, devilish, cruel, and malignant.

Man's spirit undergoes a change; he has become a partaker of the Satanic nature, spiritual death, and he dies spiritually.

He suddenly becomes a hater of God; his whole nature is rebellion toward God.

He loses fellowship and legal standing with God.

He loses his love and receives hatred and revenge; he loses his faith and receives hesitating, halting, stumbling unbelief.

He loses his rest, peace, and joy.

> *He is driven from the garden*
> *With no approach to God,*
> *Save with bleeding sacrifice*
> *Whose blood drips on the sod.*

When God created man He gave him the choice of eating the fruit of either the Tree of Life or of the Tree of the Knowledge of good and evil.

One would have united him with God; the other, with the Devil.

One would have given him Eternal Life and immortality for his body; the other, spiritual death and mortality for his body.

Adam had the privilege of becoming God's child; he forfeits it and becomes the Devil's.

Adam's Legal Right to Sell

Did Adam have a legal right to barter his dominion?

Yes, though we question that he had the moral right.

This answers these age-old questions: Why has God not disposed of the Devil if He has the power to do it; why has He permitted Satan to rule the earth and cause so much misery, if He is God Almighty.

Adam evidently had a legal right to transfer this dominion and authority into the hands of the enemy. God has been obliged through the long period of human history to recognize Satan's legal standing, and legal right and authority, and on this ground, and this only, can we understand the legal side of the Plan of Redemption.

SATAN'S DOMINION

We have come to one of the most interesting features in the Plan of Redemption, Satan's Dominion over Creation.

We have shown how Satan obtained this authority; let us now note some facts in regard to it.

The careful student of the Scripture will notice the perfect Justice of God.

He is Almighty, but He has never taken advantage of Satan.

Adam had legally transferred to him the Authority with which God had invested him.

This Authority was Time-limited.

Had God not been absolutely just He would have dispossessed Satan and punished Man then, but instead of that His Grace makes provision for Humanity's Redemption, showing His Love to Man, based upon perfect Justice.

We remember that when Jesus began His ministry, directly after He was baptized He was led away by the Spirit into the wilderness to be tempted of the Devil.

The Devil said to Him, "If Thou be the Son of God, command this stone to become bread"; Jesus said unto him, "It is written that man shall not live by bread alone."

Then the Devil led Him up and showed Him all the Kingdoms of the inhabited earth in a moment of time.

This he might have done by simply pointing to the Roman Eagle, the badge of Rome's world power.

And the Devil said to Him, "To Thee will I give all this authority, and the glory of them; for it hath been delivered unto me, and to whomsoever I will, I give it. If Thou therefore wilt worship before me, it shall all be Thine."

Now mark, Satan came to Jesus and declared to Him that the authority and glory of the inhabited earth had been delivered unto him and that he could give it to whomsoever he willed.

If the Devil lied to Jesus and Jesus did not know that he lied, Jesus was but a man and not the incarnate Son of God as we have believed. If the Devil lied to Jesus and Jesus knew he lied; then it was not a genuine temptation.

We believe that the Bible is true and it was a bona fide temptation.

If that be true, then Jesus recognized that Satan had authority and dominion over the kingdoms of the human race, authority which he could transfer at will to whomsoever he wished.

This is a hideous fact to contemplate: That the human race has been under the Dominion of the Devil, that his Dominion is a legal Dominion, and that God is unable to break it until such time as the Adamic lease, so-called, expires.

Jesus, moreover, not only recognizes Satan's authority at the opening of His ministry but also speaks of him in John 14:30 as the "prince of this world."

A literal rendering would read like this: "Now is the crisis of this world; now shall the prince of this world be cast out."

Satan here is recognized as the political head of the human race and of the kingdoms of the world.

It does not seem necessary to attempt to defend this point.

In 2 Cor. 4:3-4, "And even if our gospel is veiled, it is veiled in them that perish; in whom the god of this world (or age) hath blinded the minds of the unbelieving, that the light of the gospel of the glory of Christ, who is the image of God, should not dawn upon them."

Satan is called the "God of this world."

Here he takes his position in bidding for the worship of man in competition with the Father God.

Jesus plainly declares that men are either worshiping God or the Devil.

Paul leads us to understand that the entire world is either worshiping God through Jesus Christ or worshiping Satan.

When we realize the extent of Satanic worship in this country, our minds are staggered.

DEMON WORSHIP

When we think of the mothers who are offering their children today on the altars of Satan, on the altar of the Dance Hall, on the altar of the house of Ill Fame, and on the altar of the God of Gold, and of men and women who are making burnt offerings to the God of Nicotine daily, it makes us shudder.

It is not in India, Africa, and China alone that Satan is being worshipped, but the unhappy fact is that every land that does not worship God through Jesus Christ is a devotee of the Devil.

In John 8:44 Jesus brings another phase of this truth before our minds with awful vividness.

He is contrasting two fathers: His Father and the Jew's spiritual father.

They had lost their temper with Jesus and had said some very unkind things, when Jesus said to them, "Ye are of your father the Devil, and the lust of your father ye will do. He was a murderer from the beginning and standeth not in the truth, because there is no truth in him. When he speaketh a lie, he speaketh of his own: for he is a liar, and the father thereof."

Here we face one of the most solemn facts of the human experience, not only a fact, but an explanation for the phenomena of sin.

Man is spiritually in union with the Devil.

He has become a partaker of the Satanic nature, for Paul tells us that "we are by nature children of wrath."

John tells us "in this are manifest the children of God and the children of the Devil."

Man at the dawn of human history became a partaker of Satanic nature. That nature was breathed into his spirit by the Devil, and man became a subject of Satan.

This is the only satisfactory explanation for the power of the Devil in the world.

Satan is declared to be a murderer and a liar: the two outstanding characteristics of the human race are lying and murder.

Deny it as much as we will, ignore it if we can, the fact remains that deception and murder are the chief characteristics of the human race.

Jesus describes as a murderer a man who hates.

Hatred and revenge are deified in all great novels and dramas.

Satan is not only the Prince of this world, the God, and spiritual Father, but Paul also tells us in Hebrews 2:14 that he has the power or authority of death.

Paul tells us in Acts 26:18 that his commission was to go and deliver men out of "the authority of Satan."

John tells us that the whole world lieth in the embrace of the evil one.

These facts are unpleasant; no one would care to write them. Everyone would shrink from telling his dearest friend of them unless duty compelled it.

Man's Condition

Let us in a word sum up man's condition.

First, he has become mortal, a subject of the Devil.

He is giving birth to children not for God, but for the glory and joy of the Devil.

Second, he has become an heir to misery, pain, sickness, and death.

He is a partaker of a nature that makes him an enemy of God, and since his treason he has had no approach to God except over a bleeding sacrifice, through a God-appointed priesthood, or by dreams, or visions, or angelic visitations.

His mind has become blinded by the Devil; his nature is enmity to God, not subject to the law of God.

His eyes have been blinded to the will of God. Paul sums up his case: without covenant claims on God; without God, Godless; without Hope, hopeless; and in the world with the authority of death in Satan's hands, with no legal approach to God and no legal rights in prayer, a criminal, outlawed by his own Treason.

Questions

1. What kind of a being did God create when He created man?
2. What scripture reveals the type of mind that Adam had?
3. What dominion did God give to Adam? Give scriptures.

4. What was man's most sacred responsibility?

5. What was the nature of man's sin?

6. What was the effect of man's treason upon creation and humanity?

7. What incident in the New Testament reveals Satan's legal dominion that was given to him by Adam?

"I am a puny part of the great whole
Yes; but all animals condemned to live
All sentient things born by the same stern law,
Suffer like me, and like me also die
The vulture fastens on his timid prey
And stabs with bloody beak the quivering limbs;
All's well it seems for it
But in a while
An eagle tears the vulture into shreds
The eagle is transfixed by shafts of man
The man, prone in the dust of battlefields
Mingling his blood with dying fellow men
Becomes in turn the food of ravenous birds
Thus the whole world in every member groans
All born for torment and for mutual death."
— Voltaire

(The above reveals the dominion of Spiritual Death over all creation.)

Chapter The Third

THE DOMINION OF DEATH

HE Bible is a mystery book until we find the key that opens it; then it ceases to be a mystery and becomes a message.

There are two words that open the Bible.

The two words hang on the same key-ring.

They are the words, Life and Death.

It is impossible to receive a coherent conception of God's message without a full understanding of these two mighty words.

Sin, as we understand it today, is not the reason for Redemption; it is but one of the results of a basic cause, and until we understand that basic cause, there will be no intelligent grasp either of Man's condition or of God's provision for his Redemption.

Death has been a mystery in all ages.

Science stands mute in its presence, unable even to attempt an explanation.

Philosophy turns poetical when it meets this dread enemy of the human.

Theology has only dealt in generalities when attempting to explain it.

That bloodhound-like foe began its dread work at the cradle of the human and has followed it·down through the stream of the centuries.

It is not a part of the Creation or a part of God's original plan.

It has ever been the enemy of the human.

Man Is a Spirit

Before we can understand the Nature of Death, it will be necessary to look at the Nature of Man for a moment.

Man is a spirit and possesses a soul and has a body.

His soul and spirit constitute his personality.

Above this soul is he, himself, spirit.

This is the real Man.

This spirit operates through the soul, and it in turn operates through the physical body.

The Man and his Soul live in a body.

At death the Man and his Soul leave that body and go to their home.

It has always been difficult to realize that Man is a spirit instead of a physical being.

Paul in speaking to the Thessalonians says, "And the God of peace himself sanctify you wholly; and may your spirit, and soul, and body, be preserved entire, without blame at the coming of our Lord Jesus Christ."

The real world powers today are spiritual.

God is a spirit.

Man is a spirit.

Satan is a spirit.

KINDS OF DEATH

There are several kinds of Death mentioned in the Scriptures, but we are interested only in three, Spiritual, Physical, and Eternal (which is called "The Second Death").

The real Death is that which lays hold of our spirits rather than our bodies.

Physical Death is but a manifestation of its parent.

"The Second Death" is the ultimate finality of Death, the Home of the Spiritually Dead.

The reader will find it very difficult to think of Death except in relation to the Physical.

Physical Death is the dissolution of the physical body.

In Job 18:13 it is called "the first born of Death."

In other words primal Death is not Physical but Spiritual.

Spiritual Death came to the earth first.

It manifests itself in the Physical by destroying it.

The Physical Death is but a manifestation of a law that is at work within the human, called by Paul "The Law of Sin and of Death."

But before we take up the question as to the nature of Spiritual Death it might be well to look at Life.

There are four kinds of Life, Vegetable Life, Animal Life, Human Life, and Spiritual Life or Eternal Life.

Jesus tells us in John 5:26 that all Life heads up in God.

He is the Author of all Life whether animal, vegetable, human or Eternal, and He has given to the different kingdoms life to fit their spheres.

In other words Life is the Nature of God.

Life is the substance, the being of God.

God is a Spirit; consequently His life is Spirit Life.

Satan is a spirit, but his nature is the very opposite of God's.

God's Nature is Life, and its first manifestation is Love.

SATAN'S NATURE

Satan's Nature is Death, and its first manifestation is Hatred.

Spiritual Death, then, is as much a substance, a force, a fact as Life, but the difference is it emanates from the Devil, while Life emanates from God.

Satan was originally in heaven with God, one of those spirits who stood next to the Throne itself, but he turned against God, and when he did his Nature changed.

It is that Nature which serves as the very fountain of all that is evil, wicked, and corrupt in the human.

We can see that if all that is good, holy, and beautiful heads up in Life — which emanates from God, then all that is evil and bad and corrupt heads up in spiritual Death, which emanates from Satan.

Death, then, is a Nature as really as life is a Nature.

We can understand that out of God's Nature flows love, joy, and peace, and out of Satan's Nature comes hatred, murder, lust, and every unclean and evil force in the world.

There is no solution of the human problem without an understanding of these two super-natural forces, Spiritual Life and Spiritual Death.

If Man is dead in spirit, that is, if he is a partaker of the Nature of the Devil, then we understand his need of Eternal Life.

When God placed Man in Eden, he had the inherent power of choice and responsibility.

If he had not been created thus, he would have been an automaton, a machine under the direction of his Creator.

If this had been so, Man could have brought no more joy to God than a machine could bring to its inventor.

God gave Man not only the power of volition but also knowledge and wisdom beyond anything we have today.

He had been brought into being to be the associate and companion of the great Creator God.

That in itself indicates Man's mental and spiritual capacity.

When he was given control of the Universe God warned him, told him that if he disobeyed he should surely die, or literally "in dying thou shalt die."

This statement suggests the fact that Man is subject to a two-fold Death.

The moment Adam committed High Treason he died in spirit, but he did not die physically for nine hundred and thirty years.

It is very noticeable that the moment Man sinned His Nature underwent a complete change.

This change has no parallel in Nature except in that which is known as the New Birth, for when one is born of God he undergoes as instantaneous a change.

This proves to us that Man was actually Born Again when he sinned. That is, he was born of the Devil. He became a partaker of Satanic Nature just as man today becomes a partaker of Divine nature when he is born of God by accepting Jesus Christ.

THE NEW TESTAMENT VIEW OF SPIRITUAL DEATH

Romans 5:12, "Therefore, as through one man sin entered into the world, and death through sin; and so death passed unto all men, for that all sinned."

Through one man's sin Death entered into the world.

The picture is of Death standing outside a closed door, man's sin is throwing the door open and allowing Death to come in to the human.

This is not Physical Death, as we see in the verses following, for they say that "Death reigned from Adam until Moses," indicating at the time of Moses that there was a cessation, in part at least, of the Dominion of Death.

We know that nothing in Moses' day kept men from dying physically. It has no reference to that, but it does have reference to another kind of Death. The remainder of the chapter proves this, for in this section of Romans Paul is contrasting Spiritual Death and Spiritual Life.

That word "reign" really means "reigned as king"; so we understand that Death reigned as king over the human race from Adam's day until Moses'.

In Moses' day God gave to him the Atonement of the blood of animals.

Blood represents Life, and Atonement means a covering. So God through the High Priesthood gave to the Jewish Nation and to the Gentile world, if they wished it, a Covering of Life. Through this we understand how Death's Dominion as a world Emperor was broken.

Perhaps the most graphic statement in regard to Spiritual Death is in the 17th verse.

A literal translation reads, "for if by the trespass of one, Death seized the Sovereignty through the one."

Here is an awful picture; away back there in the Garden of Eden Death, that hideous monster seized the Sovereignty, the Dominion, the Kingship over Creation. It drove Life out and brought in its own rule of desolation. Then again in the 21st verse the same translator translates "that as sin reigned as king in the realm of death, even so might grace reign as king through righteousness unto Eternal Life, through Jesus Christ our Lord."

Here we have the truth stated clearly: Death has seized the Sovereignty, and God's Creation is under its Dominion.

We understand that sin so prevalent today, scourging and blighting the human race, reigns as king in this awful realm of Spiritual

Death where the whole human race lives today under the cruel Emperor Satan.

This is the only explanation for the present power of sin in the world.

We could not explain sin otherwise.

Sin is the outgrowth of Spiritual Death.

Spiritual Death is the soil out of which all kinds of sin grow just as Spiritual Life, the Nature of God, coming into Man becomes the soil out of which all kinds of good actions spring.

The Nature of Spiritual Death

It can be clearly seen now that Spiritual Death is the Nature of the Devil and that Spiritual Life is the Nature of God, ·that out of Spiritual Death come hatred, jealousy, and murder, and that out of the Nature of God come love, forgiveness, and peace.

We can understand now the prevalence and power of sin in the world.

We may legislate all we please; until we change the Nature of Man, sin will grow and flourish; we may stop it here or there, but it will surely spring up elsewhere.

The only hope of the human is to give him a new Nature.

Spiritual Death, then, is the Nature that lies behind all sin committed.

Man commits Sin, because his Nature produces that kind of conduct.

Spiritual Death made Man mortal.

Spiritual Life alone can make him immortal.

That was a sad day for the human when Satan became Emperor of the Universe and let loose that hideous miasma of Hell, Spiritual Death.

Power of Death

What an awakening for Adam.

He had been God's under-ruler and king.

Perfect beauty had gladdened his eyes at the rising of every sun, but now devastation has begun; the marks of Satanic Dominion are manifest everywhere.

Spiritual Death has changed the Nature of all the Animal Kingdom, and the discordant cries of Hatred and malice are heard from wooded dell to open glade; carcasses of insects and beasts lie rotting in the sun; and Adam, the uncrowned king of Creation, grovels under the iron heel of Satan.

Spiritual Death becomes a hideous reality to him; his first born son murders the second. He is made to feel with keenness the effect of his treason; he had not only sinned against God but also against his unborn children.

A little grandchild is born into the family, and Adam names it Enosh, which means "mortal," "frail," "subject to Death," or "Satan ruled."

Think of naming the first grandchild of the human race after his sin!

Man is now united with the Devil.

He is an outcast, an outlaw driven from the Garden with no legal ground of approach to God.

He no longer responds to the call of God; he responds only to his new master.

Now we understand why Man is more than a transgressor, more than a law-breaker. Man is spiritually a child of the Devil.

Man partakes of his father's nature.

This explains why Man cannot be saved by conduct.

If he is ever to be saved, it must be by some one's paying the penalty of his treason and giving him a new nature. He can never stand in the presence of God as he is.

Man is lost today not because of what he does but because of what he is. Man needs a New Birth, that is, Life from God, because he is spiritually dead.

Spiritual Death Is Universal

"And He (Christ) shall destroy in this mountain the face of the covering that covers all people and the veil that is spread over all the nations; He shall destroy death forever and the Lord Jehovah shall wipe off tears from all faces and the reproach of His people shall He take away from off the earth for Jehovah hath spoken it." Isaiah 25:7-9.

This covering that covers all peoples; this veil is the veil of Spiritual Death.

Now mark, it says here that it is a covering over all people, a veil that is spread over all nations.

Romans 5:12 declares "death passed upon all men, for all sinned."

Matt. 4:16 says, "the nations that sit in darkness shall see a light and they that sat in the shadow of death to them did light spring up."

Romans 3:9, 23 declare "that all are under sin," and "all have sinned and fall short of the glory of God."

From these Scriptures it is clear that the human race is universally under the dominion of Satan, that they have all become partakers of his Nature.

They have no legal right to approach God, and Satan is now their God and ruler.

Jesus in speaking of this in John 5:24-25 says, "He that heareth my word, and believeth Him that sent me, hath eternal life, and cometh not into judgment, but hath passed out of death into life."

Jesus is speaking of the spiritually dead who by hearing His voice may come out of the Realm of Death into the Realm of Life, out of the family of Death into the family of Life.

In the story of the Prodigal Son Jesus makes the father say, "This is my son that was dead and is now alive, was lost and is found."

In 1 John 3:14-15 it says, "We know that we have passed out of death into life, because we love the brethren. He that loveth not abideth in death. Whosoever hateth his brother is a murderer, and ye know that no murderer hath eternal life abiding in him."

Here we have the contrast of Death and Life: that is the contrast of the manifestation of the Nature of the Devil and the Nature of God; one manifests itself in hatred, and the other, in love.

"And you did he make alive, when ye were dead through your trespasses and sins,

"Wherein ye once walked according to the course of this world, according to the prince of the powers of the air, of the spirit that now worketh in the sons of disobedience:

"Among whom we also all once lived in the lusts of our flesh, doing the desires of the flesh and of the mind, and were by nature children of wrath, even as the rest: but God, being rich in mercy, for His great love wherewith He loved is, even when we were dead through our trespasses, made us alive together with Christ (by grace have ye been saved)." Ephesians 2:1-5.

Let us look critically at this section of Scripture: first, we were made alive when we were dead.

Second, we walked according to the prince of the powers of the air.

Third, this prince is now working in the sons of disobedience just as the Holy Spirit works in the sons of obedience.

Fourth, we all once lived in the lusts of our flesh and were by nature children of wrath.

Fifth, but God being rich in mercy, for His great love wherewith He loved us when we were dead in our trespasses made us alive together with Christ.

Take this statement with Col. 2:13, "You being dead through your trespasses and the uncircumcision of your flesh, you, I say, did He make alive together with Him, having forgiven us all our trespasses."

From these Scriptures the case is made: Man is spiritually dead, under the dominion of the prince of the powers of the air, and this spirit is now working in and through man's life carrying out the plans and purposes of this prince.

All this substantiates our foregoing argument: the universal man must be Born Again, and the New Birth is receiving the Life or Nature of God. John tells us that when we receive this Nature we love our brethren, and he that does not receive this Nature has hatred for his brethren.

THE CONTRAST

Here Again Death and Life are contrasted.

In Romans 8:1-14 Paul contrasts the Flesh and the Spirit, Life and Death.

In verse two, "For the law of the spirit of life in Christ Jesus made me free from the law of sin and of death."

The law of sin and of death is that law that is at work today in the realm of Spiritual Death, mentioned in the 5th Chapter, and since Paul has been born again he is free from the dominion of this former ruler.

The term Flesh as he uses it indicates Man's Condition before he is made alive, or Born Again.

The Greek word "sarx" in this connection has reference to Man when he is spiritually dead.

The 6th verse, "For the mind of the flesh is death, but the mind of the Spirit is life and peace."

The mind of the flesh is the mind of the natural Man in the realm of Spiritual death, and this mind, he says in the 7th verse, is "enmity against God. It is not subject to the Law of God; neither indeed can it be."

The Man who lives in the realm of Spiritual Death is enmity against God.

He may be a college professor. He may hold the highest place in the educational world. However, if he has never been born from above, he is God's enemy by nature, and he cannot be a subject of God's Law. However, Paul says of the believer, "Ye are not in the flesh but in the Spirit, if so be that the Spirit dwelleth in you."

In other words if you have been Born Again, passed out of the realm of Death and Satanic Dominion into the realm of Life and the Spirit's Dominion, "ye are no longer in the flesh," and should not be Ruled by the senses.

You remember Paul's pathetic cry in the closing of the 7th chapter of Romans, "Wretched man that I am! who shall deliver me out of the body of this death?" Then he cries, "but I thank God through Jesus Christ I have found my deliverance."

Paul was speaking of the time when he was spiritually dead, a child of the Devil, but awakened by the Spirit to his bondage and also to the privilege of deliverance.

Summing Up the Case

Let us now in conclusion see what we have found.

First, Spiritual Death is the Nature of the Devil.

Second, Man by his sin has become a partaker of Satanic Nature.

Third, this union with Satan has separated Man from God.

Fourth, Man is now an outlaw without legal ground of appeal or approach to God.

Fifth, if Man ever stands right with God some one must pay the penalty of his transgression and give him a new Nature.

Sixth, neither Education nor Culture can ever change his Nature; the New Birth is Man's only hope.

Questions

1. What are the two words that open the Bible?
2. Name and explain the three kinds of death.
3. What is Eternal Life?
4. Explain Romans 5:12.
5. Give a discussion of the reign of spiritual death.

"The total picture of life is almost too painful for contemplation; life depends on our not knowing it too well. If we should bring clearly to a man's sight the terrible sufferings and miseries to which his life is constantly exposed, he would be seized with horror; and if we were to conduct the confirmed optimist through the hospitals, infirmaries, and surgical operating-rooms, through the prisons, torture-chambers, and slave kennels, over battlefields and places of execution; if we were to open to him all the dark abodes of misery, where it hides itself, from the glance of cold curiosity, he, too, would understand at last the nature of this best of all worlds. For whence did Dante take the materials of his hell but from our actual world?"

(The above picture of the reign of evil surely reveals the lordship over the human race of the one whom the Scriptures call "Satan".)

Chapter The Fourth

SATAN

HERE is no explanation for the intelligence and organization that is behind the power of sin, if there be no such a being as Satan.

The prevalence, power, and malignity of sin compel us to look for a cause.

To say that sin is inherent in man is to accuse God of creating a being in whose nature sin forms a part.

We cannot accept this.

If it could be proved that there were no such a being as Satan, then the difficulty of locating the seat, the fountain of sin, would be encountered.

The Scripture is explicit; it tells us as much about Satan as about God. It tells who he was and who he is today, how he became what he is, and tells us how he gained dominion over the human race.

It tells us of his malignant nature and character, tells us also of his end.

All that is holy, righteous, and good heads up in one, and all that is evil, unjust, and destructive heads up in the other.

SATAN'S LEGAL DOMINION

One of the bitterest facts that humanity and Heaven have to face is that Satan has a legal right to rule over the human race.

God gave to Adam dominion and authority.

This dominion was over Satan and over all the works of God's hands.

Man ruled not only Satan, but he also ruled all the angelic beings. He was next in authority to God, and when he turned that vast Kingdom over into the hands of Satan, it was a legal transference. It was so legal that God was obliged to recognize its legality, and the only way that God could meet the issue was to send His Beloved Son down out of Heaven to suffer the penalty of Adam's transgression.

If you will notice, all through the Scriptures God and the angels treat Satan with a certain deference; they recognize his legal dominion.

If Satan did not have legal dominion, why is it that God, who is Almighty, did not put him out of business and drive him off the earth into his eternal prison-house?

But God could not do it- Consequently there has come into being that marvelous legal document, The Plan of Redemption.

You remember that when Jesus met Satan in the Wilderness in the great temptation that Satan said, "To Thee will I give all this authority and the glory of them, for it has been delivered unto me, and to whomsoever I will, I give it; if thou therefore wilt worship before me, it shall all be Thine."

Jesus does not dispute Satan's claim; He takes it for granted that Satan is telling the truth.

Satan's bold boast and offer to Jesus is one of the striking facts of history.

Satan, then, has legal rights that God must and does recognize.

Adam had a legal right though not a moral right to transfer the dominion that God had placed in his hands into the hands of the Devil, the enemy of God.

There can be no plan of redemption nor theological system that does not recognize Satanic dominion. There can be no excuse for God, if this dominion is not a legal dominion; for if God has a legal right to dispossess the Devil and put him out of dominion and does not do it, He necessarily becomes guilty of all the acts of the Devil.

However, if man with his free moral agency and the legal rights that have been conferred upon him by God turns that dominion into the hands of his enemy, God has no right to dispossess the Devil until man's lease of dominion has expired.

Who He Is

This is a study of the Being who is today ruling the earth, who sits as the Prince of the Nations, who has the Authority to rule the hearts and lives of men, who is the author of all our miseries and sorrows; the Being who has the power of disease and death, and Authority to cast into Hell.

He is the King of the angels of the Abyss; he rules the dark hosts of Hell.

His chief desire and design is to destroy the human race and thereby bring sorrow to the heart of the Father God.

In Luke 10:18 Jesus says, "I saw Satan as lightning cast out of Heaven."

In Isaiah 14:12-15 he is called the "Day Star, Son of the Morning," and his Fall it attributed to his desire to rule the Heavens and cast God out.

He said, "I will ascend into Heaven; I will exalt my throne above the Stars of God; and I will sit upon the mount of congregation in the uttermost parts of the north; I will ascend above the heights of the clouds; I will make myself like the Most High."

This with Ezekiel 28:11-19 gives us a hint of who Satan was.

The 28th chapter of Ezekiel is addressed first to the Prince of Tyre, who is serving under his great Emperor, Satan.

Satan is described as having the dominion over the earth, over the Kings of the earth — this is a picture of Satan's ruling a nation through its King.

Beginning with the 12th verse we see him in his true light: "Thus saith the Lord Jehovah: Thou sealest up the sum, full of wisdom, and perfect in beauty."

This description cannot apply to any man living at the time of Ezekiel, for it says, "Thou wast in Eden, the garden of God."

We know that Satan was there.

"And every precious stone was thy covering," as the precious stones in the crown of a King are his covering the insignia of his office, of his authority.

And so God says that "The sardius, the topaz, the diamond, the beryl, the onyx, the jasper, the sapphire, the emerald, and carbuncle and gold" are in that wonderful covering or crown.

And then He says, "The workmanship of thy tabrets and of thy pipes was in thee; in the day that thou wast created they were prepared.

"Thou wast the anointed cherub that covereth: and I set thee, so that thou wast upon the holy mountain of God: thou hast walked up and down in the midst of the stones of fire.

"Thou wast perfect in thy ways from the day that thou wast created, until unrighteousness was found in thee."

The being whom God is describing here (and it is God who is speaking) is a being perfect in beauty, summing up perfection and wisdom, and was the anointed cherub.

The word "anointed" suggests that he was connected with the throne, and the reference to musical instruments, that he evidently led the worship of Heaven; he led the great angel chorus in their worship of God.

He was able to walk up and down in the very presence of the Eternal God, and he was perfect in all his ways until unrighteousness was discovered in him.

"Therefore have I cast thee as profane out of the mountain of God: and I have destroyed thee, O covering cherub, from the midst of the stones of fire.

"Thy heart was lifted up, because of thy beauty; thou hast corrupted thy wisdom by reason of thy brightness."

This could only apply to a heavenly being who held a place of authority, and glory and honor before God Almighty, and whom God cast out from His presence.

When Satan was cast out of Heaven, he evidently lost none of his ability or brilliancy, and none of his wisdom; it simply became corrupted.

Passion Music

It is a significant fact that music today holds a large place in all the brothels, dance-houses, theaters, and operas and that music is one of the attractive features of sin today.

Satan has not ceased to be a musician; neither has he ceased to lead great choruses and oratorios.

In Revelation 9:11 he is called the King, the angel of the Abyss. His Hebrew name is Abaddon, and his Greek name is Apollyon. He is the great King of the demon hosts of Hell.

He is the mighty Enemy of God today; he is an enemy of angels and of men.

He heads up all the evil of all the ages.

According to the scriptures he has the power of disease, the power of death, the power to bring plagues upon humanity, the power to cause storms and unnatural fires.

His whole nature is malignant and cruel.

He evidently loves the esthetic and beautiful; his fall did not take that from him.

Whenever he has an opportunity he uses these to destroy and wreck the spirits of men.

THE PRINCE OF POLITICIANS

Luke 4:3-7, "And the Devil said unto Him, if Thou art the Son of God, command this stone that it become bread.

"And Jesus answered unto him, It is written, Man shall not live by bread alone.

"And he led Him up, and showed Him all the kingdoms of the world in a moment of time.

"And the Devil said unto Him, To Thee will I give all this authority, and the glory of them: for it has been delivered unto me; and to whomsoever I will I give it.

"If Thou therefore wilt worship before me, it shall be thine."

Here Jesus recognizes that Satan has the political dominion over the kingdoms of the earth and that the whole human race are his subjects.

In a previous chapter we called attention to the means by which Satan obtained this dominion.

Here Jesus recognizes his right to rule.

As the Prince he is the political head of the nations.

I don't believe that any one can doubt this. When we look at the history of the human race, the corruption of our cities, of our politics, of the rulers of the great nations of the earth; when we consider the awful wars and massacres that take place in semi-civilized countries with a tacit recognition of the great nations of the earth, we are convinced of Satan's reign.

Jesus calls Satan the spiritual father of the human race: "Ye are of your father the devil:" and He was speaking to the Jews, the most religious and the best people of the world at that time.

Paul tells us that Satan is the god of this world.

As the father he has given man his nature; as the god he demands man's worship, reverence, and obedience; and that he has it we can't deny.

Satan is more popular today than Jesus; Hell is more popular than Heaven.

More people go the Broad Way than the Narrow.

More people worship the Devil than worship God.

THE AUTHORITY OF DEATH

Jesus tells us in Luke 12:4-5, "Fear him, who after he hath killed hath authority to cast into Hell: yea, I say unto you, Fear him."

Jesus declares that Satan has the authority of death and the authority to cast into Hell.

Hebrews 2:14, "Since then the children are sharers in flesh and blood, he also himself in like manner partook of the same; that through death he might bring to nought him that hath the power of death, that is the devil."

Here Paul tells us the same thing, that Satan has the authority of death.

This seems a hideous fact, that the authority of death, to slay men, is in the hands of our Enemy.

In Revelation 12:7-9, "And there was war in Heaven: Michael and his angels going forth to war with the dragon: and the dragon warred and his angels: and they prevailed not, neither was their place found any more in Heaven.

"And the great dragon was cast down, the old serpent, he that is called the Devil and Satan, the deceiver of the whole world; he was cast down to the earth."

The earth is Satan's realm; here he rules over demons and nations.

The ninth verse of Jude tells us that arch-angels respect the Devil and show him a peculiar reverence.

Zech. 3:1-2, "And he showed me Joshua the High Priest standing before the angel of Jehovah, and Satan standing at his right hand to be his adversary."

"And the angel of Jehovah said unto Satan, Jehovah rebuke thee, O Satan; yea Jehovah that hath chosen Jerusalem rebuke thee: is not this a brand plucked out of the fire?"

Here the angel of Jehovah dares not directly rebuke Satan, but shows him a peculiar respect and honor.

Satan is greater than any angelic being in Heaven; only God and Jesus Christ are greater.

Demon Dominion

Daniel 10:13, "But the Prince of the kingdom of Persia withstood me one and twenty days; but Michael one of the chief princes, came to help me."

Daniel had been praying for one and twenty days and wondered why his prayers were not answered.

Suddenly an angel appears and makes the statement that he had been held up one and twenty days by the Prince of the kingdom of Persia. It was not a human Prince, because no human could have intercepted an angelic being, but a demon who was ruling over the kingdom of Persia had stopped him on his way to Babylon to bring God's message to Daniel.

The angel also makes another declaration.

He says that he is going back now to fight with this same Prince of Persia, indicating that every kingdom is ruled by a demon. Paul declares that our combat is not against flesh and blood but against principalities and powers and world rulers of this darkness; that there are different degrees of demoniacal dominion; and that the world is divided up into kingdoms and states, and communities, and that over each one a demon holds sway.

This, I have become convinced, is true, for in my evangelistic work I find a different kind of demon in almost every community.

This is uncanny and an unpleasant subject, but nevertheless it is imperative that the Church know about it.

In 1 John 3:10 and John 8:44 he is called the spiritual Father of the human race: "Ye are of your father the devil," and, "In this are manifest the children of God and the children of the devil."

1 John 5:19, "The whole human race lieth in the embrace of Satan."

He has a peculiar dominance over the nations of the earth.

It would seem that Revelation 12:11 is being fulfilled, that Satan has already come down to this earth full of wrath, knowing that his days are short.

His Character

We can best understand Satan's nature in the same way that we understand God's, that is by his Names.

The whole series of revelations of God in the Old Testament are revelations through the Names that He gives. Therefore, we will study the names of our great Adversary, Satan, in order to discover his character.

"When any one heareth the word of the kingdom and understandeth it not, then cometh the Evil One, and snatcheth away that which hath been sown in the heart." Matt. 13:19.

Here he is called the Evil One of the earth.

Verses 38-39 of the same chapter. "And the field is the world: and the good seed, these are the sons of the kingdom; and the tares are the sons of the Evil One; and the Enemy that sowed them is the Devil: and the harvest is the end of the world; and the reapers are the angels."

Here he is called the Devil and the Father of the tares.

He not only steals away the good seed that is sown in the hearts of men, but he also sows tares and wickedness in the world.

His name "Devil" means "Accuser," "Defamer," "Calumniator," "Slanderer."

These are titles that describe his character.

The very word "Devil" has enwrapt within it all the significance of these four synonyms.

He Is the Accuser

He accuses the brethren day and night before God.

He is the Defamer; he is defaming the Church, and the character of God; and the integrity of Jesus continually.

He is the Calumniator; he is ever bringing railing accusations, vile, unclean accusations against the human.

He is the Slanderer; he retails all that is vile and unclean.

He stirs up dissensions; bitter awful scandals are the delight of this archfiend.

It would be well for us to stop here and notice this fact: neither God nor Satan can minister to or destroy the human but through the human.

He Uses Man

Satan must use human lips or pen to do his dirty work for him.

He has no power to defile, to destroy, or to lead astray, except as he has a human instrument.

God has no power to bless, to inspire, to lift, to save men except through a human instrument.

It seems a crowning pity that man should lend himself to the Devil as a medium through which he can work to destroy the human race, but he does it.

In 2 Cor. 11:3 he is called the Corrupter, "But I fear, lest by any means, as the serpent beguiled Eve in his craftiness, your minds should be corrupted from the simplicity and purity that is toward Christ."

Here Satan is the corrupter, the defiler, the robber of virtue and the purity of the heart.

Satan has always delighted in being the instructor of youth.

He uses some vile man or woman to defile a boy or girl and then sends that boy or girl out as a missionary into our public schools and colleges to defile the minds of the innocent.

How often our sweet baby boys and girls are corrupted and robbed of their purity of heart before they reach the high school grades; nothing is left holy or pure to them.

The holy secrets of life are all dragged into the filth and mire of vile conversation and suggestions, and our sweet babies come back to us scarred forever by Satan's defilement.

1 Thess. 3:5, "For this cause I also, when I could no longer forbear, sent that I might know your faith, lest by any means the Tempter had tempted you and our labor should be in vain."

Here he assumes a new guise, the Tempter.

He is the sly serpent, tempting Eve from her purity; and Paul fears that the virgin Church of Thessalonica shall be tempted from her love and fidelity to her Lord.

He is called the Seducer.

No name is so vile in our English as that, and Satan is known as the Seducer of the virtue and purity of the Church of Jesus Christ.

He is vile, sly, and cruel, the old serpent.

In Rev. 20:2 is a constellation of names that are hideous to contemplate, "the dragon, the old serpent, which is the Devil and Satan."

PASSION DANCE

Perhaps the name of all names here is "the old serpent."

The word "serpent" really means the fascinator, and how truly Satan has fascinated men and women of all ages since the Fall.

He has given to us the ball-room with its fascinating body-gripping passion music, imported to us from the South Sea Islands, from Cuba, and the Negroes of the South, music that throbs and pulsates with a passion that stirs all that is worst in fallen man.

It is no wonder that 90 per cent of the girls today in the houses of ill-fame in this country went there through the public dance hall.

There is nothing that so un-mans a man and a woman and throws them open to the God of Lust as this subtle passion music of today.

Satan has reached his highest point of fascination in this subtle, dangerous type of music.

He could only reach a few through the so-called classical music, but passion music is based on one of nature's perverted fundamental laws.

However, the dance hall is not the only place where he fascinates.

There is the card table over which $80,000,000 pass daily, where men blow their brains out, where they throw manhood and character to the winds, where they barter love and home.

And not only does he fascinate with cards and the dance-hall but also with the theater and moving pictures, and today they are holding out a fascination that is emptying our Churches, wrecking the students in our schools, and destroying the boyhood and the girlhood of the nation.

Oh, Satan is a fascinator!

As the bird is fascinated by the serpent, so is the girl and the boy, the man and the woman fascinated by the "old serpent" today, and they walk with closed eyes and benumbed sensibilities into his very jaws.

In Col. 1:13 he is called the "Power of Darkness" out of which we are "translated into the kingdom of the Son of His love."

Darkness stands for ignorance; ignorance has ever been Satan's choicest weapon to keep in bondage the great hordes of humanity.

He has held the hosts of the earth's great family in bitter, soul-blighting ignorance.

Not only has he bound with ignorance, but he also has given them a fear of light so that they fight the force that would set them free.

The light hurts their eyes.

The battle between Light and Darkness has gone on down through the ages.

The darkness tried to overcome the light during the days of the Incarnation.

Oh, the bitter sins of darkness, the unnumbered sins of darkness!

Darkness is really the realm of Satan.

But I want you to look once more at the hideous constellation of horror in Rev. 12.

Here he is called the Dragon, the Devil, the father of hatred, the father of murder, the Adversary, the Old Serpent whose deadly coils have crushed the life out of nation after nation and proud city after proud city, until tonight their only monument is the wreckage of their past glory that we see in the piles of their mighty ruins.

SATAN'S REPUTATION

John 8:44, "Ye are of your father the Devil, and the lusts of your father it is your will to do. He was a murderer from the beginning and standeth not in the truth, because there is no truth in him; he is a liar and the father of lies."

Here Jesus gives Satan a reputation that is not enviable.

He is called a murderer from the beginning, and stands not in the truth for there is no truth in him; he is called a liar and the father of lies.

Perhaps the badge of the unregenerate human today is the lie.

The human race are liars!

Lying is as natural as eating or drinking or breathing.

To overcome lying is one of the most difficult things that any man or woman ever attempted.

We lie in dress, in our appearance; we lie in our speech; we lie with our eyes, with our hands, with our pens; we lie with words, and without words; we lie in business, and in the pulpit.

Satan is truly a murderer of characters, and then he covers his awful tracks with a series of fabrications most malicious, but that does not seem to be his worst name; he has another honorary degree.

He is called in Revelation the Deceiver of the whole earth.

This is to me the bitterest fact that we have to face in connection with the Devil, that he has deceived the whole inhabited earth, that no man lives or has lived, who has not been fooled and deceived by Satan.

He has made sin appear beautiful; he has made error seem as truth, lust as love, crime as virtue, and deception as good policies.

He deceives the babe, the youth, and young manhood.

He deceives us in the prime of life; he deceives us on the brink of the grave when faltering footsteps seek for a guide.

He has deceived us as a world, as nations, as cities, as schools, as homes, and as individuals.

Satan is humanity's Nemesis.

From the cradle to the grave he has sought to utterly destroy the human.

His master stroke is compelling man to carry out his wicked design against God and God's eternal purpose for man.

Man is helpless without God's aid to escape his power.

SATAN'S TIME-LIMIT

There are those who have believed that the Time of the Gentiles began with Nebuchadnezzar's dominion, that is, the Gentile's world dominion.

We know that the Greek word for Gentile means nations, and when Jesus in Luke 21:24 speaks of the Times of the Gentiles being fulfilled or the Times of the Nations, He has reference to a wider interpretation of humanity than this limited view will admit.

Paul, speaking of the same thing in Romans 11:25, says, "that a hardening in part hath befallen Israel, until the fullness of the Gentiles be come in," the fullness of the Gentiles being the fullness of the nations.

We know that the nations of the earth are under the dominion of the Devil, and Jesus and Paul both evidently have reference to the end of the Satanic dominion.

When Jesus began His ministry and began to cast out demons, we have record of a remarkable statement made by a demon which He was casting out.

In Matthew 8:29, demons cried, "What have we to do with Thee, Thou Son of God? art Thou come hither to torment us before the time?"

Again in Rev. 12:12, "Therefore rejoice, O Heaven, and ye that dwell therein; woe to the earth and sea, because the Devil has gone down to thee with great wrath, knowing that he hath but a short time."

From these and other Scriptures we learn that Satan recognized that his dominion was time-limited.

It would seem then that when God gave Adam dominion over the earth and the work of His hands that this dominion was limited as one of our modern leases is limited.

Adam had dominion over the earth for a certain number of years, whether it be six or seven thousand, or how long, we do not know.

When Adam committed High Treason against God and turned this dominion and authority over into the hands of Satan, Satan took Adam's lease, and consequently Satan's dominion will last as long as Adam's would have lasted had he not sinned.

It is evident that Satan's dominion ends at the Second Coming of the Lord Jesus.

The dominion of man is really now the dominion of Satan, or as Paul puts it, "the Times of the Gentiles," or of the nations, which is the time of Satan's dominion over the human race.

The demons that were cast out by Jesus knew their time-limit, and they dreaded being cast into the Pit or Abyss before their time. They appealed to His justice and said, "Hast Thou come to cast us into the Abyss before our time?" And Jesus said, "No, I will not do it."

In the scripture just quoted it says that Satan will come down to the earth with great wrath knowing that the days of his authority are numbered.

That will give a reason likely for The Great Tribulation which ends this dispensation.

Satan, as he sees the hours of his dominion over man draw to a close, will pour out his bitterest vials upon the human race to hurt God and crush humanity before he is finally cast into the "Lake of Fire."

We are living today in the days of Satan's dominion, but thank God, there is a time-limit to it.

Here are some facts about Satan that will aid us.

First, He was an angel of light and led the worship of Heaven.

Second, He was "The anointed cherub that covereth," stood near the Throne.

Third, He fell by trying to take the Throne from God.

Fourth, He was perfect in beauty and wisdom.

Fifth, He lost none of his wisdom.

Sixth, His nature was changed by his fall.

Seventh, Adam gave him Dominion over the Universe.

Eighth, He Rules Earth and Man.

Ninth, He has power to bring storms, pestilence, wars, disease, and death.

Tenth, He is seeking God's place in our hearts; he wants our worship.

Eleventh, He has access to God to accuse the Church.

Twelfth, He is to be bound and cast into Hell at Christ's coming.

Thirteenth, At the Judgment he goes into the "Lake of Fire," and that ends his awful reign.

Questions

1. What is the only explanation for the intelligence and organization that there is behind sin?

2. Discuss Satan's position before he was cast out of heaven.

3. What facts of history unveil the reign of Satan as god of this world?

4. Show how Satan's character is revealed through the names that are given to him in the scripture.

5. In whose hands is the power of death? Give scriptures.

"The loving, the gentle, the sympathetic, the sacrificial Savior, who loved sinning men so that He came to die for them — He, calmly, deliberately, over and over again, did teach His disciples in such a way that they at that time and since then the great body of the church have believed that He meant us to understand that there is a future state of punishment, and that it is so great and dreadful a thing that all men should with terrible earnestness flee from it.

"He announced the fact. He did not reason upon it, nor point out its place in a system of moral truth, nor give it philosophical definition, nor consider objections to it, nor attempt to reconcile it with any theory of divine power. He raised His hand to the sky to draw aside the curtain, and there, right before His hearers rose the dark grandeur of future Retribution. He bore witness to it as a fact.

"When I doubt the teaching of Hell, therefore it will be because I doubt the Divinity of Christ."
— Henry Ward Beecher.

Chapter The Fifth

HELL

IF there be a Hell, a place of confinement, a prison for the incorrigibly wicked, it matters not the nature of it, it will be a place of torment.

Under the most humane conditions possible in this century in which we are living, a prison is a prison, and it is horrible even to contemplate.

What we want in this discussion is to know what the Word of God teaches in regard to the state of the wicked after death.

It may be interesting for us to notice this, that Hell is the jail where the wicked are locked up when under indictment until the court sits and their sentences are passed on them; then they go into what is called in Revelation the Lake of Fire, the Gehenna of the New Testament.

The Lake of Fire is the Federal Prison of Eternity; Hell is simply the County Jail.

No one has yet been put into the Lake of Fire.

The wicked angels and wicked men are both locked up today in Hell, awaiting the resurrection of the wicked and the Judgment, after which they go to the Federal Prison.

You know that Heaven is not the permanent abode of the Believers; it is merely a tentative place to which the disembodied spirit goes to await the return of the Lord Jesus and the first resurrection when the Believer will receive his immortal body. He is then ready to enter into the New Heavens and the New Earth, where he will dwell in an immortal, physical body with his beloved ones through Eternity.

When the sinner dies today, he, in his spiritual form, goes to Hell to remain there until the Second Resurrection when his old body will be raised full of sin, disease, and corruption.

He will enter it again and stand in that physical body before the great White Throne of God. Jesus Christ will be Judge. Then the dread sentence will be passed according to the Court's findings, and he will be sent away with the Devil, the False Prophet, and the fallen angels into the Federal Prison of Eternity.

The reason for Hell and the Lake of Fire is apparent to every thinking man.

Eternal Criminals

Man is an Eternal Being. He belongs to the same class as God. If he dies a criminal, then he enters Eternity as an eternal criminal.

There must be a prison; the criminals must be segregated.

If they were permitted to roam indiscriminately through Eternity, they would demoralize the New Heavens and the New Earth.

We have jails, State Prisons, and Federal Prisons for time criminals who break the laws of man.

Who can raise a protest against God if He has a prison in which are incarcerated the men who violate the laws of Heaven, and who are eternal criminals?

The Universal human believes in some kind of Hell and place of confinement for punishment after death, and this testimony is not easily ruled out of court.

There is no type of testimony so convincing to a jury and judge as the testimony of universal human consciousness.

There must be some basis of fact for this universal belief.

All primitive peoples believe that the Good go to some kind of Heaven and that the Evil go into confinement.

We may believe in a literal Lake of Fire and Brimstone or that the term is only used to illustrate the torture and misery of confinement and separation from God.

A Prison Is A Prison

The fact is: to be locked up in a Federal prison away from your loved ones with the loss of freedom and with a consciousness that all your mortal days are to be spent behind those walls, knowing that God's great big out-of-doors is forever closed to you, that no longer can you go where you wish or come when you please, that you have lost the power of volition and of action and that a guard with a gun walks up and down the concrete corridor before your steel-barred doors in a uniform that becomes hateful to you is Hell enough for any man.

If this is to last through Eternity, God help me, I want to evade it.

I don't need the fumes of sulphur, nor the creeping, biting, burning worms of Hell described in the Scripture.

To be shut in with the incorrigibly wicked through Eternity, to be associated with the blasphemers and murderers, with the whoremongers, the liar, the thief the dissolute women of all ages, never to see a pure face again, never to hear a baby's prattle, never to hear a hymn of praise or the folklore songs of love, to hear nothing but bitter, biting, hideous blasphemy, the gnawing of the tongue, the gnashing of teeth, the biting agony of long confinement is all that is necessary to make it Hell for me.

As for me, let me escape it; let me never be in danger of it.

MEANING OF THE WORD

The word for Hell in the Hebrew is Sheol.

There are many synonyms as Rephaim, the Shades, the Pit, the Lowest Deeps, but the word "Sheol" occurs seventy-six times in the Old Testament.

The Greek word of the New Testament is Hades; there are several synonyms used in the Greek meaning the same place.

The Hebrew word means "Mansion of the Dead," "the Invisible Abode," and "Place of Punishment," "the lowest place or state," or, as another puts it, "the prisons of the Incorrigible," "the place of restraint."

The reason for Hell has been suggested in my introduction; let me state it again.

Man is eternal; angels are eternal.

When men and angels become criminals, they become eternal criminals.

Since man is an eternal criminal, there must be a place for eternal restraint.

Man is a spirit, and there must be a spirit home for man.

Since man is a criminal, and traitor, a jail is imperative, and after Judgment the Federal prison is a necessity.

Hell was not made for man.

It was prepared for the Devil and his angels.

Heaven and earth were the places prepared for man.

God has been compelled through man's sin to build, in spite of love, a place of confinement for Eternity's criminals.

God intended originally that man should live on the earth eternally. It was made for this purpose, and man was made with an eternal body; but when he sinned and became mortal, Hell had to be fitted for his confinement.

God did not intend originally to ever separate man from his body; so Heaven can never be considered man's final Home.

Man's final home must be a place where he can dwell in a physical body eternally either in confinement or blissful liberty.

Hell and the Grave

There are some teachers who have industriously told us with pen and voice that Hell and the Grave were synonymous terms.

The reason for this error, for error it is, is that the King James Version erroneously translates the word "Sheol" thirty-five times as "Grave."

When they translated it, there was not the knowledge of the Hebrew language that we have gained in this last century.

We know that there are many errors in this translation that have made it imperative that a new translation be given to the world, and I look upon the American Revision as the very best, and recommend it to every zealous Bible reader to use in preference to the King James Version.

The use of a word in either the Hebrew, the Greek, or in our English, determines its meaning, and it will be interesting to notice how the word "Sheol" is used in its seventy-six places in the Old Testament.

We wish to compare it with the word "Queber" which means Grave or Sepulcher, and by this comparison it will be very easy to determine whether the two words can be used interchangeably or not.

A Vital Contrast

The word "Sheol" is never used in the plural: the word "Queber" is used in the plural twenty-nine times.

The word "Sheol" is never located on the surface of the earth; "Queber" is located on the surface of the earth thirty-two times.

Bodies are never put into "Sheol" by man, but bodies are put into "Queber" thirty-seven times.

No individual has a "Sheol" of his own, but individuals have "Quebers" forty-four times.

Man never puts another man into "Sheol," but man puts man into his Grave or "Queber" thirty-three times.

Man never digs a "Sheol"; man digs a "Queber" six times.

Man never touches "Sheol," but it speaks of man's touching "Queber" five times.

By this we see that the word "Sheol" is never used interchangeably nor in the sense of Grave where the human body is placed by man.

It is never used synonymously with the word that we translate grave or sepulcher, and by its use it is very clear that "Sheol" and "Queber" are not the same, and that "Sheol" cannot be translated grave.

The translators of our American Revision saw this, and instead of translating the word at all, they simply put it in the English untranslated.

The one who tells you that the Grave and Hell are synonymously used is either ignorant of the use of the words and their meanings in the Scripture, or else he is dishonest.

We would prefer to feel that he is ignorant.

The Nature of Hell

A very vivid picture of Hell is given in the 14th of Isaiah where it describes the death of Nebuchadnezzar, the great Emperor of Babylon, and his descent into Hell.

"Sheol from beneath is moved for thee to meet thee at thy coming; it stirreth up the dead for thee, even all the chief ones of the earth; it hath raised up from their thrones all the kings of the nations." Isaiah 14:9.

It would seem that Satan was preparing a great reception for the world Emperor, Nebuchadnezzar, that he had raised up the thrones of all the kings and they sat upon them with their officers and slaves gathered about them in Oriental splendor.

Then down from the upper world is brought the great Nebuchadnezzar, the world's greatest Ruler.

He is suddenly ushered into the presence of these kings and princes sitting upon their mock thrones.

They all answer with one cry, "What? Hast thou fallen as low as we? Is the majesty of thy greatness and the music of thy singers brought down to Hell? Art thou as weak as we?"

This wail of lost men, of kings and princes, of generals and great financiers, sitting on their mock thrones in pitiable agony and helplessness meets the ear.

"The worm is spread under thee," they cry, "and worms cover thee," crawling fiery serpents, coiling and uncoiling about the spirit of the great Nebuchadnezzar.

He has made kingdoms desolate; he has slain the mother with her babe; he has crushed nation after nation; he has put out eyes of kings and princes; and now in a horrid Hell he writhes in agony, and his agony is witnessed by the assembled multitudes, many of whom he sent there.

In Isaiah 66:24, it speaks of Hell as a place where the "fire is not quenched, and the worm shall not die, an abhorrence to all flesh."

Daniel tells us that the resurrection of the wicked shall be a resurrection of shame and contempt.

According to Matt. 25:41, 46, it is the home of the cursed, the eternal fire, which was prepared for the Devil and the rebellious angels. Now it has become the jail and home of the wicked human; it is called the place of eternal punishment or constraint; a place out of which no pardoned has yet gone or ever can go; no pardon can reach them, horrible as it may seem.

In 2 Peter 2:4, it is called the pit or prisons of punishment, and in Rev. 9:1-2, it is a place of fire of sulphuric fumes, the home of demons; but in Luke 16:19-31 Jesus gives us a picture of Hell that only He could give.

This is not a parable; it is not placed among the parables.

He says, "A certain rich man;" he is quoting history, and He gives a description of Hell and of torment, of conscious intelligible torment that surpasses Dante in his Inferno, or Milton in his Paradise Lost.

It would be well here to note this fact: that during the period from the fall of man until Christ ascended and took His place at the right hand of the Father on high after His resurrection, the Underworld was in two compartments with an impassable gulf separating them.

On one side were the Old Testament saints who had trusted in the Blood Covenant, the Abrahamic Blood Covenant; so it is called by Jesus "Abraham's bosom."

Across this impassable gulf the incorrigibly wicked were incarcerated awaiting the resurrection, and Judgment.

It would seem evident that when Jesus arose from the dead, and had carried His blood into the Holy of Holies in Heaven, and had satisfied the claims of Justice in the redemption of the transgressors under the first Covenant, that He again went back down into what is known as Paradise and preached to the souls waiting there, and carried to them the good news of redemption, and they with Him ascended up to Heaven, for as far as we know, no human beings had gone into Heaven, unless it was Elijah.

No one could go there, because the sin problem was not yet settled; they only had a promise of redemption written in the blood of bulls and goats.

Jesus came to die for the sinner under the first Covenant; so that they who were called should receive their portion of the inheritance.

So we can understand this picture in the 16th of Luke.

"Now there was a certain rich man, and he was clothed in purple and fine linen, faring sumptuously every day; and a certain beggar named Lazarus was laid at his gate, full of sores, and desiring to be fed with the crumbs that fell from the rich man's table, yea, even the dogs came and licked his sores.

"And it came to pass, that the beggar died, and that he was carried away by the angels into Abraham's bosom; and the rich man also died and was buried.

"And in Hades he lifted up his eyes, being in torments, and seeth Abraham afar off, and Lazarus in his bosom.

"And he cried and said, Father Abraham, have mercy on me, and send Lazarus, that he may dip the tips of his finger in water, and cool my tongue; for I am in anguish in this flame.

"But Abraham said, Son, remember that thou in thy lifetime receivedst thy good things, and Lazarus in like manner evil things, but now here he is comforted, and thou art in anguish.

"And besides all this, between us and you there is a great gulf fixed, that they who would pass from hence to you may not be able, and that none may cross over from thence to us.

"And he said, I pray thee therefore, father, that thou wouldst send him to my father's house; for I have five brethren; that he may testify unto them, lest they also come into this place of torment.

"But Abraham saith, They have Moses and the prophets; let them hear them.

"And he said, Nay, father Abraham; but if one go to them from the dead, they will repent.

"And he said unto them, If they hear not Moses and the prophets neither will they be persuaded, if one rise from the dead."

We understand this story to be a purely Jewish story. There is no Paradise today, but there is a Hell.

Paradise was emptied, and all its inhabitants taken to Heaven.

This rich man went to Hell, because he had broken the fundamental principles of the Mosaic Law: He did not love his neighbor as himself.

The whole law was summed up in this: Thou shalt love the Lord, thy God, with all thy heart, and thy neighbor as thyself.

This he had broken and was paying the penalty for it.

Now I want you to notice some significant facts in regard to man as he goes to Hell.

"And in Hades he lifted up his eyes, being in torment."

Notice that he has all the faculties of the soul.

Man is not a physical being, he is primarily a spirit.

His tongue was burning in that intense heat, "For I am in anguish in this flame."

Whether we want to insist that this is purely figurative language or not, is beside the question.

The fact is that Jesus declared that this man was in torment in the flames.

If the flame was simply a burning conscience, then give me literal fire.

"Son, remember;" the man remembered.

Memory lives in Hell.

Two things will haunt man in Hell and fill him with sleepless agony.

First, the sins that he has committed against God and man; and second, that he had an opportunity to escape it, but he resolutely preferred Hell to Heaven.

Hell is here a place of anguish, with the great gulf fixed so that there is no passing over from one to the other.

There is no second probation promised here.

The man who is guilty enough to be sent to Hell is guilty enough to stay in Hell.

Then we come to the most pathetic thing.

He said, "Will you not send Lazarus up to earth? I have five brothers there, lest they also come into this place of torment."

Oh, the unspeakable pathos of this hopeless request!

What a preacher a soul would make, fresh from the agonies of Hell, but men would not listen to his message.

Some of the most intelligent men that we have in this country believe that if they can keep the subject of Heaven and Hell and the sufferings of Christ from their minds, or stay away from places where they hear it preached, that they will escape the responsibility of knowledge and that in itself will prove their salvation from Hell.

Oh, how fallacious is that dangerous sophistry!

But the answer came, "They have Moses and the prophets, let them hear them."

"Nay, father Abraham, but if one go from here up there, him they will listen to."

But did they?

Jesus went from Hell's dark dungeons and fiery awful sufferings up to earth and gave His testimony, but have men heeded it?

Nay, verily! Men ridicule it today.

WHO GOES TO HELL

Thank God, we do not believe that babies go there.

We trust, though we could not prove it from Scripture, that all infants until they come to the age of accountability are saved on the ground of the finished work of Christ.

Personally, I have no doubt in regard to this.

Psalm 9:17 says, All the nations that forget God are cast into Hell, that the fearful and unbelieving are cast into Hell.

Every man who refuses to recognize the Lordship of Jesus Christ or confess Him as Savior will go to Hell.

There is no distinction; "Unless a man is born from above, he cannot enter the Kingdom of God; he will enter the Kingdom of Satan.

There will be no educational test, no philanthropical test, no financial test; the man who is not sheltered by the sacrifices of Jesus Christ will go to Hell as surely as does the Devil.

Man does not go to Hell because of what he has done, but because of what he is.

Man goes to Hell on purely intellectual grounds; he can evade it if he wishes.

He goes to Hell today in the face of modern civilization with his eyes wide open, and because he prefers Hell to Heaven.

He goes there, because he has served Satan, and because he prefers Satan as his god to the God and Father of our Jesus Christ.

Sin is more attractive to him, and Hell, more desirable than Heaven is.

Questions

1. Are Hell and the Lake of Fire synonymous terms? Give reason for your answer.

2. Why must there be a place of confinement for spiritually dead man?

3. Show why Hell and the Grave as used in the Hebrew and Greek are not synonymous terms.

4. Who will go to Hell?

5. Why will no one sent to hell be able to accuse God of injustice?

It also presents God to you as reconcilable through a Mediator. In that Gospel "peace is preached to you, by Jesus Christ. That Gospel lets you see God in Christ reconciling the world unto Himself, that sin may not be imputed to them. The Gospel proclaims glory to God in the highest, peace on earth, goodwill towards men. So did the voice of angels sum up the glad tidings of the Gospel, when that Prince of Peace was born into the world. It tells you God desires not the death of sinners, but that they may turn and live; that he would have all men be saved, and come to the knowledge of the truth." — John Howe.

(Man today has no approach to God except through this Mediator Jesus Christ. "For there is one God, one mediator also between God and men, himself man, Christ Jesus," 1 Tim. 2:5.)

Chapter The Sixth

MAN'S NEED OF A MEDIATOR

I N the preceding chapter we found that man is a legal outlaw; he has lost his approach to God and is described by Paul in Eph. 2:12: "separated from Christ, alienated from the commonwealth of Israel, strangers from the Covenants of the promise having no hope, without God in the world."

Notice first, "alienated from Christ;" there is no life, no approach to God but through a mediator, and man has no mediator.

Second, he is a stranger from the Covenants of the promise.

Man has no covenant claims on God; he has forfeited every right which God has conferred upon him.

God had given him legal rights of approach and a standing before him.

These, by his treason, he forfeited, and now his position is described as having no hope and without God in the world.

Hopeless, Godless, and in the world where Satan has the power of death, man's position is certainly desperate.

But more than this, man is described in my previous chapters as having become a partaker of satanic nature.

He is not only a subject of Satan politically, but he is vitally unioned with him; so he is described as "by nature a child of wrath," spiritually dead, and a child of the Devil.

By these descriptions, man's case is absolutely hopeless.

Man has no ground for prayer.

If God hears his prayer, it is on the ground of grace alone.

Man's condition is described in Exodus· 33:20, "And He said, thou canst not see my face, for man cannot see me and live."

The testimony of universal human consciousness is that from the fall of man until Jesus Christ sat down at the Right Hand of the Father no human being has ever approached God but through a divinely appointed priesthood, over a bleeding sacrifice, by dreams, by visions, or angelic visitations.

The universal man recognizes that he has no legal standing with Deity.

The temples, altars, and priesthoods of all nations eloquently confess man's consciousness of sin, and fear of death and of Judgment to follow.

The universal man fears death; the universal man believes in a Judgment and punishment for guilt after death.

Perhaps no more eloquent testimony on this phase of the theme could be offered than the black hopelessness of the heathen lands.

India with its millions of priests struggling in absolute hopelessness, is but one of many.

None of the old religions of the world have any real hope, or solution of the sin problem, or of man's ability to approach God without fear.

The human condition can be summed up in these awful words:

No Hope!

The mind reels at the stroke;
The dying flame, the trembling frame,
The ashen lips that spoke.
No hope!

No hope!
Earth's language of despair;
The aching heart, the bitter part,
The soul's sad solitaire.
No hope!

No hope!
The heart shrinks from the gloom;
The darkling cloud, Sin's awful shroud,
Comes with the sinner's doom.
No hope!

No hope!
The winter blast of death;
Its icy kiss, the dark abyss,
There's frost upon its breath.
No hope!

No hope!
No hope in Jesus.
The death knell of the soul:
No hope, no hope in Jesus,
While endless ages roll!

No Hope!

Job in a very graphic way gathers up the dirge of human hopelessness in his great master poem.

As Goethe caught the inspiration from the folk lore of the Germanic people and gave it to us in Faust, so it has been the privilege of some seer or poet to be the voice of his people at different periods of human history.

Job is not the poet of a single people, but the poet of the human, the poet of the ages, and his theme can be called the question of the ages: "How can man stand right with God?"

The sages and philosophers of all the ages have asked this same question in one form or another.

You remember that the book of Job is the oldest of all the books of the Bible.

It was written evidently by Jobab, a cousin of Abraham, about the time that Jacob went into Egypt, and the portions that I read to you will show how live a subject was "Man's Need of a Mediator" in Job's day.

Turn to Job 4, beginning with the 12th verse; here we have a picture of an Arab lying in his tent in an oasis in the desert.

The night is cool and chill; the heavens are clear, and the stars like jewels are sparkling through the midnight air.

The man is lying in his tent asleep; suddenly he is disturbed by a vision; let us read; "Now a thing was secretly brought to me, and mine ear received a whisper thereof. In thought from the visions of the night, when deep sleep falleth on men, fear came upon me, and trembling, which made all my bones to shake.

"Then a spirit passed before my face; the hair of my flesh stood up. It stood still, but I could not discern the appearance thereof; A form was before mine eyes: There was silence, and I heard a voice, saying, Shall mortal man be just before God? Shall a man be pure before his Maker?"

This is the old problem; this is the eternal problem that has confronted the thinking man of all ages: Can mortal man be justified or acquitted before God? Shall fallen man be pure in the presence of his Maker?

You will remember that the word "mortal" applies only to the physical body, never to the spirit, and that in both the Hebrew and the Greek, it means "death-doomed," "frail;" in other words, a subject of the Devil.

Jesus was not mortal until He became our sin substitute. Now the problem is: Shall a mortal man, or a death-doomed man, or a Satan-ruled man, that is, one of Satan's subjects, stand uncondemned in the presence of God?

In the 9th Chapter of Job there is a graphic picture of an aged man on his death-bed facing the problem of eternity with all his faculties quickened by the near approach of Judgment.

Job is now speaking out the deepest soul agony of universal man.

Let us see the picture, A man lying in a tent surrounded by those whom he loves, and he opens his heart with perfect freedom speaking out the fears that grip his soul in the death struggle.

He cries, "My days are swifter than a runner. They flee away; they see no good. They are passed away as a swift ship, as the eagle that swoopeth on her prey."

These are all figures of speech describing the rapidity with which days and months and years pass to the aged.

Were we speaking today we would speak of the express train, the speeding auto, the hurtling airplane as it shoots across the face of the sun, swifter than a bird, all telling in living words how rapidly days and months dissolve into each other to the aged.

He continues, "If I say I will forget my calamity; I will put off my sad countenance and be of good cheer, I am afraid of all my sorrows. I know that Thou (God) will not hold me innocent; I shall be condemned."

Conviction has laid its relentless grip upon his mind.

Sorrow of approaching Judgment gathers in dark clouds over his spirit.

The last sun of hope is rapidly setting in the evening of darkness.

Not one ray of light penetrates the gloom of his tent.

Every false hope has been shattered; he is alone with his sin, his guilt, and his despair, and he says, "What is the use of trying to brighten up and put off my sad countenance; I am afraid of my sorrows."

It is the darkness of despair; it is the hopelessness of full-orbed knowledge, "I shall be condemned."

He knows it, and then in almost petulant despair, he cries, "Why do I then labor in vain, why spend my time making garments of fig leaves? If I wash myself with snow-water, and make my hands ever so clean; yet wilt Thou plunge me in the ditch and mine own clothes shall abhor me."

Here are convictions and a consciousness of guilt that cannot be smothered; it must give vent to itself.

Its agony is the outgushing torrent of stifled convictions of years at last getting fair play.

What a picture! "Thou wilt plunge me in the ditch and mine own clothes (or self-righteousness) shall abhor me; for He is not a man, as I am, that I should answer Him, that we should come together in judgment."

Job knows that he cannot face God, for God is not mortal. He is not under the bondage and guilt of sin as Job is. Then he utters the saddest words that ever fell from the lips of a human.

"There is no umpire betwixt us that might lay his hands upon us both."

In other words, there is no Mediator betwixt us who has a legal standing with God and at the same time can sympathize and understand as well as represent the human.

This is Job's cry for a Mediator; and it is not the cry of Job alone, for Job has gathered up the cry of the ages and breathed it forth in one hopeless sob.

How bitterly he says, "Let Him take His rod (His law), away from me, and let not His terror make me afraid; then would I speak with Him face to face, but now I am not able."

Job has voiced Man's Need of a Mediator.

"How then can man be just before God? or how can he be clean than is born of woman? Behold, even the moon hath no brightness, and the stars are not pure in His sight: How much less man, that is a worm! And the son of man, that is a worm!" Job 25:4-6.

This sounds almost like the New Testament: "How can he be clean who is born of woman?"

The writer here has the fall of man through Eve before his mind, and when he tells us that the stars are not pure in the sight of God, he is referring us to Adam's treason in which he turned creation over into the hands of the Devil, allowing Satan to defile it so that God cannot look with joy upon it.

In speaking of man as a worm, he shows the depths into which man has fallen. The worm has reference to Satan, the Old Serpent, and man here who is a worm is spiritually a child of the Devil, utterly hopeless and without approach to God.

It might be interesting to read Jer. 30:21 in this connection, "And their prince shall be of themselves, and their ruler shall proceed from the midst of them and I will cause him to draw near and he shall approach me; for who is he that hath had boldness of heart to approach unto me? saith Jehovah."

Or, as it reads in the margin, "Who hath surety for his soul that he might approach Me."

Jeremiah recognized that no man had a right to stand in God's presence, nor power to do it, and he tells us that there is one being who will be able to draw near and stand uncondemned in God's presence, our Mediator, Christ.

This gives us a picture of the utter despair, the perfect hopelessness of the human race, and mark you, it is a legal hopelessness.

Man is a legal criminal, and if he ever stands right with God it must be done on legal grounds.

Now we can understand more clearly the reason for the great religions of the world.

All thinking men have sought and are seeking today a solution of the sin problem and grounds whereby man can stand uncondemned in the presence of God.

You read in Gen. 3:9-10, 22-24, "And Jehovah God called unto the man, and said unto him, Where art thou? And he said, I heard thy voice in the garden and I was afraid, because I was naked; and I hid myself."

"And Jehovah God said, Behold, the man is become as one of us, to know good and evil; and now, lest he put forth his hand, and take also of the tree of life, and eat, and live forever — therefore Jehovah God sent him forth from the garden of Eden, to till the ground from whence he was taken. So he drove out the man; and he placed at the east of the garden of Eden the Cherubim, and the flame of a sword which turned every way, to keep the way of the tree of life."

Adam was unable to stand in God's presence after his sin; he was finally driven from the garden, and a flaming sword was placed at the gate so that man could not get to the tree of life.

God would not permit man to eat of the tree of Life until the sin problem had been settled.

It would have been an awful thing had God permitted man to eat of the tree of Life while under condemnation of treason. He would have had a dual nature.

Let me give you some illustrations of man's attempting to force himself into the presence of God before Eternal Life came through Jesus Christ, and Justification on the grounds of His finished work.

Leviticus 10:1-3 is one of those pathetic acts of Divine Justice that was necessary in order to cause Israel to know its spiritual condition before God.

"And Nadab and Abihu, the sons of Aaron, took each of them his censer and put fire therein and laid incense thereon and offered strange fire before Jehovah, which He had not commanded them. And there came forth fire from before Jehovah, and devoured them, and they died before Jehovah. Then Moses said unto Aaron, This is it that Jehovah spake, saying, I will be sanctified in them that come nigh me, and before all the people I will be glorified. And Aaron held his peace."

What a calamitous closing of the dedication of the priesthood.

Aaron and his family that morning had been aspiring to the highest point of divine favor; the tabernacle had been reared; the Shekinah presence had filled it with glory; the majesty of Jehovah was resting upon Israel.

Behind them lay a series of divine interventions or miracles that had marked them as the chosen people of the God of the whole earth. Now Aaron's firstborn, heir to the priesthood, with his brother, is suddenly smitten with death before the whole congregation.

What has occasioned it?

Moses and Aaron at the close of the morning services had gone to their tents for the mid-day meal.

These two sons had been lingering near the tent of meeting where the holy Ark of the Covenant had been placed, and the presence of Jehovah was abiding there.

The young men, in a spirit of bravado or curiosity, take up censers with live coals, pour incense upon them, and attempt to enter the Holy of Holies without being invited by Jehovah and contrary to law.

No one but the High Priest himself could go in there, and he, but once a year.

Suddenly the young men stagger, stumble, and fall back across the threshold, dead.

A cry goes up from those who are looking on.

Messengers run to the tent where Moses and Aaron are and tell them of the awful calamity.

Poor Aaron stands horrified, shocked, stunned in the presence of his dead.

Moses cried to him, "Aaron, this is what Jehovah spoke, saying, I shall be sanctified in them that come nigh me, before all the people will I be glorified."

And Aaron held his peace.

Israel had learned by this awful Judgment that man could not approach God except in His own appointed way.

We have another example of man's attempting to approach Jehovah unauthorized in Numbers 16.

It is the bitter story of Korah and his rebellion.

Korah and a company of the leaders of Israel became jealous of Moses and Aaron and insisted that they had as much right to approach Jehovah as had God's appointed priests.

Moses put the issue to a test in the presence of the whole congregation.

He invited Korah and his followers to appear before Jehovah with their censers ready to worship, and as soon as they came Moses warned the people to get up from the tents of these wicked men who dared to approach God uninvited and in their own way.

No sooner had Moses ceased speaking than the earth opened its mouth, and the fifty men with their families dropped down alive into Sheol.

Israel ran frightened from the awful scene, filled with fear and reverence for such a Holy God.

Another illustration is given us in 1 Sam. 6:19; the Ark of the Covenant had been captured because of Eli's great Sin.

It had been taken down into Gath by the Philistines, and after a series of Judgments had fallen upon the heathen cities because of their desecration of the Ark, they put it on a cart and sent it back to Beth-Shemesh.

The cattle drawing the cart turned off from the road into the fields.

When some of the people laboring in the field saw the Ark, the news spread rapidly over the hillsides till thousands and ten thousands of people gathered from the country around about, reverent and curious.

Then a bolder spirit than the others drew near and threw off the heavy covering from the Ark of the Covenant, and the people for the first time saw that holy receptacle of the Ten Commandments.

Suddenly a plague struck them, and fifty thousand men fell dead upon the ground.

Awful fear and consternation fell upon the people. Beating their breasts, they turned back to their homes.

Israel had learned a lesson: that no one can approach God but through a High Priest or over a bleeding sacrifice.

God's character has not changed.

Fallen man's nature is the same.

Man today can no more approach God without a Mediator than he could in the days of Israel.

Men tell us that if they live a good moral life, that is, pay their debts, do by men as they should do, that this is all God can require of them, and that if there is a Heaven they have as much right to it as those who trust in the merits of Jesus of Nazareth.

Men who say this are either ignorant of the history of the human race, of its long agonies under the burden of sin, of its many attempts to have a conscience cleansed of guilt, of its priesthoods and altars, its sacrifices and prayers; or else they are self-deceived and mentally blinded by the god of this age.

The nations that have not embraced Jesus Christ have steadily sunk lower and lower since His birth nineteen hundred years ago.

Only the people who have welcomed Him as Savior and have received the Life that He brings from God have shown improvement in the Sciences, Arts, Mechanics, and Morals.

Let no one deceive you.

Education will not fit a man to stand right with God. Job shows a mental culture and knowledge that is not surpassed today by any of the great European Savants.

David shows intellectual development that none of the great educators can surpass.

Isaiah shows a chastity and fine discrimination along the highest intellectual lines that is not equalled by any writer that the nations have produced in the last thousand years.

These writers all teach one great truth: "Man needs a Mediator."

Today, scholarship if it is scholarship, knowledge if it is real knowledge, should lead all minds to the same goal: "Man needs a Mediator."

Humanity's hopeless wail, sung in the minor of its uncomforted misery is heard in every generation; "How can man stand right with God, or how can he be pure that is born of woman?" Man needs a Mediator.

Questions

1. Discuss man's condition as revealed by Eph. 2:12.

2. How does history reveal that universal man recognizes that he has no standing before God?

3. How does Job express man's need of a mediator?

4. Give two experiences of Israel that reveal that man cannot approach God in his own way.

5. Why is man's need of a Mediator just as great today as it ever was?

"We know now that God is like this that we have seen in Jesus. He is Christlike. And if He is, He is a good God and trustable. If the Heart that is back of the universe is like this gentle Heart that broke upon the cross, He can have my heart without qualification and without reservation. I know nothing higher to say of God than that He should live like Christ. 'The question to my mind,' said a Yale professor, 'is not as to the divinity of Jesus but as to whether God will act like Jesus.' Strange, a Man lived among us, and when we think of God we must think of Him in terms of this Man, or he is not good. We may transfer every single Moral quality in Jesus to God without loss or degradation to our thought of God. On the contrary, by thinking of Him in terms of Jesus we heighten our view of God. All those who have tried to think of Him in other terms have lowered and impoverished our idea of Him. — E. Stanley Jones.

Chapter The Seventh

THE INCARNATION

OR

THE HUMANITY AND DEITY OF JESUS

HE question of the Humanity and Deity of Jesus was contested more bitterly during the early days of Christianity than almost any other question.

It has been the battle ground of speculators, metaphysicians, philosophers, and theologians.

Jesus puzzles them.

To the natural mind He is a mystery; no man has ever produced such startling results in the human.

He changed liars to truth-tellers, lazy men to workers, thieves to honest men, caused corrupt society to become clean, wholesome, and safe.

In China today thousands of the Literati, Mandarins, principals of academies and Colleges, political leaders, officers in the army, and heads of the local governments are turning to Jesus Christ, and the miracle is that it changes their lives, their hearts.

There is something in this man Jesus that changes one's nature the moment one takes Him as his Savior and crowns Him Lord.

What is it?

The writer knows what it is by experience.

Most of the readers likely know what it is.

Now what is there about this man Jesus that makes Him and every man who embraces Him so different?

You may read Shakespeare, and it does not change your nature.

You may study the works of any man, and your nature will not be changed by it, but you cannot embrace Jesus as your Savior without having a miracle performed in your spirit.

Why is this?

It lies in the fact that Jesus was different.

He was not generated after the common laws of nature.

John says, "The Word was made flesh and dwelt among us and we beheld His glory, full of grace and truth" (or reality).

The Incarnation is the most striking miracle of creation; yet from Heaven's point of view and man's need it is inevitable.

An Incarnation Fact

Could the Son of God have been Incarnate if His body had been conceived by natural generation?

Would it have been possible for God to have come into a child born of natural generation and dwell in the child and be Incarnate?

We cannot see how this is possible, for Paul tells us that "All have sinned and fallen short of the glory of God," and that "death (spiritual) has entered into all men for that all sinned."

If Jesus had been born of natural generation and God had come into Him, He would have been a fallen spirit, a being subject to the Devil with God dwelling in Him; that would not be an Incarnation.

This would utterly destroy the idea of a perfect Incarnation of God.

The seed must be of divine origin instead of human.

Man is subject to the Devil; his seed only produces a fallen man.

The Incarnate One could not be a subject of death nor of the Devil; so we believe that Jesus during His earthly walk was not a subject of death, neither was He a subject of Satan.

Death had no dominion over Him until the sins of the world had been laid upon Him on the Cross, and not till then did He become a mortal being.

Jesus was not immortal, but He was a perfect human as Adam was a perfect human before the Fall.

If God could have changed the nature of a child after birth so that He could be Incarnate in the child, He could as well have changed the nature of the whole human race in the same way.

But to do this would have been an injustice to Satan and an injustice to Himself, because the sin problem had not yet been settled and the penalty of man's transgression had not been paid.

The Redeemer must be one over whom Satan had no legal claims or authority, and this could only come by a Redeemer's being conceived and born as was the Babe of Bethlehem.

The teaching of Incarnation is not out of harmony with human desire or tradition.

It has been believed in by all tribes and peoples in some form.

The Universal Man has craved Incarnation.

This is proved by man's drinking blood and by cannibalism, by the naming of his kings after the titles of his deities, and by the universal reverence of the thing offered on the altars of the gods.

Incarnation is supernatural, but all peoples believe in the supernatural.

Education cannot eliminate man's fundamental yearning for and belief in the supernatural.

Incarnation is God's answer to the cry of the Universal Man for a visit of Deity to the earth and for a union with Deity.

Incarnation means that Deity has become united with humanity in an individual.

The Incarnation is the only solution of the human problem.

Since the fall of man the human has steadily been sinking lower and lower intellectually, morally, and spiritually, and the only hope is for Deity's union with humanity to bring man back to his lost estate.

The Incarnation should be desired by every sane man when he understands it, for it offers to humanity a hope, and without it man is hopeless.

Every false religion that denies the Incarnation of Jesus of Nazareth has attempted to provide a theory of universal Incarnation in order to stimulate to a higher moral and spiritual life.

Theosophy tries to make us believe that all men have the nature of Deity.

The same thing is held by practically all our modern liberal theological teachers and preachers! That the so-called "Spark of

Divinity" dwells in all men, that the New Birth is simply the awakening, the blowing-into-a-flame, of this spark of Divinity.

If man had a spark of Deity or any part of Deity abiding in him, then man was already God Incarnate.

We know that this theory is fallacious, for humanity has experimentally proven it false.

The entire New Testament contradicts it.

If we accept any of the Bible, we must accept it all.

The Incarnation of Jesus of Nazareth is no more difficult to believe nor to understand than the creation of the first man or the birth of a child.

If God is Almighty, He had power to beget a child in the womb of the Virgin Mary.

If Jesus was Incarnate, Man and God can become united; God can dwell in these human bodies of ours; God can impart His own life and nature to our spirits, and we may have God's life in these human bodies.

If Jesus was Incarnate, then immortality is a fact.

If we do receive Eternal Life for our spirits, then we have positive assurance that these bodies will become Immortal at the return of the Lord Jesus.

If the Incarnation is a fact, Christianity is supernatural.

Every man who has been "born again" is an Incarnation, and Christianity is a miracle.

The believer is as much an Incarnation as was Jesus of Nazareth.

We cannot conceive of any man's desiring to doubt the Incarnation, as it offers the only solution of life's mystery; it gives the reason for man's being; it makes life with its burdens, sorrows, and grief which culminate in death tolerable; it throws light upon this human problem that can come from no other source.

The Incarnation has been the craving of the Universal Man, and if Jesus of Nazareth was Incarnate, the universal cry has found its answer in Christianity.

The Incarnation is the basic miracle of Christianity.

It proves the Pre-existence of Christ and is the foundation and reason for all subsequent miraculous manifestations of divine power.

Man's condition demands an Incarnation, because he is spiritually dead and without an approach to God.

The Incarnation of Deity with humanity will provide a Substitute of Deity and humanity united on such a ground that the Incarnate One can stand as man's mediator, being equal with God on the one hand and united with man on the other; He can bring the two together.

Again, being Deity and humanity united, He can assume the obligations of human treason, satisfy the claims of justice, and thereby bridge the chasm between God and man.

Gen. 3:15 is God's first promise of Incarnation. It is given in His conversation with Satan just after the Fall.

"And I will put enmity between thee and the woman, and between thy seed and her seed; He shall bruise thy head, and thou shalt bruise His heel."

Let us notice four remarkable promises or statements in this sentence.

First, "I will put enmity between thee and the woman," that is, there will be enmity between Satan and the woman.

This is proved by woman's history; she has been the special object of Satanic hatred and malice in all ages; she has borne the brunt of the Fall; she has been the burden bearer among all peoples; she has been bought and sold as common chattel.

In India today she is not worth as much as a cow in the open market; only where Christianity has reached the hearts of a country has woman ever received any treatment that would lift her above the brute creation.

She is unwanted at birth, the plaything of man's passions, the neglected, the outcast, the sufferer, and in Christian countries she is the heir of our diseases and the victim of the divorce court.

Doctors tell us that 95 per cent of all the hospital cases are of the women; 22 per cent of the married women of this country suffer on account of their husband's having sowed "wild oats," and "sowing wild oats" means sowing our manhood for Satan's reaping.

"I will put enmity between thy seed and her seed: "Satan's seed is the unregenerate human race; woman's seed is Christ.

Christ was hunted from His babyhood by Satan's seed until finally they nailed Him to the Cross, and from the Resurrection of Jesus until this day, the Church has been the subject of the bitterest persecutions and enmity of the world.

Second, I want you to notice that remarkable term, "the seed of woman."

We know that woman has no seed; the seed is of the man; therefore what can this mean?

It is a prophecy that woman shall give birth to a child independent of natural generation, that it shall be called the "seed of woman."

This is not a Hebraism for the term does not occur anywhere else throughout the entire Hebrew Scriptures.

This is a direct statement of fact. That there shall be a "seed of woman," and that seed, Paul tells us, is "The Christ."

"And He shall bruise thy head," that is the head of Satan.

In all Oriental languages, "bruising the head" means breaking the Lordship of a ruler.

Satan has just come into his Dominion; he has the Dominion that God had given to man, and he is going to exercise this Dominion without any interruption until this wonderful Seed of woman comes, who is going to break his Lordship.

This is a remarkable prophecy, and how clearly it found fulfillment: first, in Jesus' bitter persecution which finds its culmination in His death on the Cross, and then in the persecution of the Church which is the Body of Christ, and which is carrying out the will of Christ on the earth.

The long ages of persecution of the Church by the seed of Satan is today merely a matter of history.

"The heel," is the Church in its earth walk.

In the 20th verse of the same chapter, "The man called his wife's name Eve, because she was the mother of all living."

The word Eve in the Hebrew is "Havvah," which literally means the living one, or the mother of the life-giver.

Here God tells man that his wife shall be the mother of life, or the mother of "the life-giving One," our Christ.

Born of a Virgin

Isaiah 7:13-14, "And he said, Hear ye now, O house of David: Is it a small thing for you to weary men, that ye will weary my God also? Therefore the Lord Himself will give you a sign: behold the Virgin shall conceive, and bear a son, and shall call his name Immanuel."

This child is going to be born of the House of David, and "the Lord Himself will give you a sign."

God Himself will show you a miracle, a wonder. Something out of the ordinary is going to take place, and we say, "What is it?"

And he says, "the virgin," as though he had marked her out, "shall conceive and bear a son, and his name shall be Immanuel."

It is a son that a Virgin is going to give birth to in a supernatural way, and she is going to call His name Immanuel, God with us, or Incarnation.

Take this in connection with Luke 1:31-36, "And behold thou shalt conceive in thy womb, and bring forth a son, and shalt call his name Jesus.

"He shall be great, and shall be called the son of the Most High; and the Lord God shall give unto Him the throne of His father David; and He shall reign over the house of Jacob forever; and of His Kingdom there shall be no end.

"And Mary said unto the angel, How shall this be, seeing I know not a man?

"And the angel answered and said unto her, The Holy Spirit shall come upon thee, and the power of the Most High shall over-shadow thee: wherefore also the holy thing which is begotten shall be called the Son of God."

This child you notice is conceived of the Holy Spirit. It is a supernatural birth.

The prophet Isaiah had looked down through the ages and had marked out Mary, the daughter of Heli of the family of David. She was a cousin of Joseph who was also of the family of David; and so the prophet exclaimed, "O house of David, is it a small thing that you weary me; I will show you a sign."

He is marking out this daughter of David, who is going to give birth to that wonderful being in a manger cradle in Bethlehem 750 years later.

Jer. 31:22, God declares, "A woman shall encompass a man," more literally, "A woman shall encompass a man-child."

This Incarnate One could not be born of natural generation, because man is a fallen being and his seed is subject to Satan.

The seed must be of one who is not a subject of Satan, and so this wonderful being must be conceived of the Holy Spirit, and the womb of the Virgin is to be simply the receptacle of that Holy thing until the day it is brought forth.

Isaiah 42:6 says, "I Jehovah have called thee in righteousness, and will hold thy hand and will form thee, and give thee for a Covenant of the people, for a light of the Gentiles."

Adam was created; the rest of the human race were generated by natural processes, but this child that is going to be born, is to be "formed" by a special act of Divine power.

Paul speaks of His birth in the following words, Phil. 2:6-8, "Who existing in the form of God, counted not the being on an equality with God a thing to be grasped, but emptied Himself taking the form of a servant, being made in the likeness of men; and being found in fashion as a man, He humbled Himself, becoming obedient unto death, yea, the death of the Cross."

Notice these terms: He had existed always in the form of God, but now He empties Himself and takes the form of a bondservant, being made in the likeness of men and being found in fashion as a man.

All these suggest a separate and distinct operation of God, different from natural generation.

Here is a being with whom God performs a miracle: first by taking Him out of the Godhead or from the Godhead in Heaven and placing Him in the womb of a Virgin to be unioned with flesh by a unique conception.

Again Paul says, "Wherefore when he cometh into the world, he saith, Sacrifice thou wouldest not, but a body didst thou prepare for me."

God prepared a body, a special body, for this being called the Son of God.

PRE-EXISTENCE OF CHRIST

Psalm 107:20 declares, "He sendeth His word and healeth them and delivereth them from their destruction;" and John says (1:14) that "The Word, (the Eternal Logos, the expression of God,) became flesh and tabernacled with us."

Paul tells us in 1 Timothy 3:16 that God "was manifest in the flesh."

Romans 8:3 says that "God sending His own Son in the likeness of sinful flesh."

Galatians 4:4-6, "When the fulness of the time came God sent forth His Son born of a woman, born under the Law, that He might redeem them that are under the Law."

The Incarnation presupposes that this being who became Incarnate had an existence previous to His coming to the earth.

Seventeen times in the Gospel of John, it is declared that Jesus was sent forth from the Father and came into the earth, and that He again left the earth and went unto the Father.

The entire Gospel of John is based upon the fact that Jesus had a previous existence with the Father, and that while He was walking the earth He remembered His experiences in the other world, and spoke to the Father of these experiences, and also of when He would go back and take up again life with the Father: John 3:16; 8:42; 13:3; 16:28, 30; 17:3-8.

Micah 5:2 is a remarkable prophetic utterance of the pre-existence of Jesus, and His coming to earth: "Out of thee, Judah, shall one come forth unto me that is to be ruler in Israel, whose goings forth are from of old, from everlasting."

Here there is one going to be born of the family of Judah to be a ruler in Israel, and His goings forth have been from of old, from everlasting.

He has traveled up and down through the eternities, and has left His foot-prints on the ages.

From these Scriptures, both prophecy and fulfillment, with the wonderful story of Jesus, the Incarnation seems a very simple and reasonable thing.

We know the reason for the Incarnation: Man is spiritually dead and a servant of Satan, and no man by natural generation could redeem him.

The Incarnation is absolutely necessary, because humanity must be delivered by a human, and any human born of natural generation must be under Satan's dominion.

Questions

1. Why is it that this man Jesus has influenced humanity as no other man ever has?

2. Why was it that man's needs demanded the Incarnation of Deity?

3. Could the Son of God have been incarnate if His body had been conceived of natural generation? Give the reason for your answer.

4. Show why the teaching of the Incarnation is not out of harmony with human desire or tradition.

5. What was the first prophecy of the Incarnation? Give several others.

"Being justified freely by his Grace through the redemption that is in Christ Jesus: whom God set forth to be a propitiation through faith in his blood, to show his righteousness because of the passing over of the sins done aforetime in the forbearance of God; for the showing I say of his righteousness at this present season: that He might be righteous and the righteousness of him that hath faith in Jesus." Rom. 3:24-26.

"So then as through one trespass the judgment came unto all men to condemnation; even so through one act of righteousness the free gift came unto all men to justification of life. For as through the one man's disobedience the many were made sinners even so through the obedience of the one shall the many be made righteous." Rom. 5:18-19.

Chapter The Eighth

HOW GOD CAN BE JUST

AN is ever accusing God of injustice in His dealings with the human race, and has declared that He had no right to create man in the face of the fact that He knew man would fall.

Man questions God's right to judge the human race and to execute sentence commensurate with the crime.

Can God justify Himself in the face of these age-old accusations?

Has God a right to send one man to Hell and another to Heaven?

Has God, as Judge, a right to execute the sentence prescribed in Scripture against the Christ-rejector?

The time has come when we must face this issue squarely.

Theorizing and speculation will not satisfy us.

The fact of a Hell we cannot deny, and we are here and cannot get rid of ourselves.

We cannot escape our responsibilities!

We are eternal personalities, and so we must face an eternal situation.

The Case

We have found in other chapters that man is the reason for creation, that every step in this wonderful drama of the human has one basic fact which confronts us at every turn, and that is, man was created to answer the yearning heart-hunger of the Great Father God.

Second, we found that man was created for joy, for happiness, and for peace; that sin, sickness, and death, hatred and revenge had no place in the original plan of the Creator; and that present conditions of society and of the world are not normal.

They never were a part of the original design: they are the products of an Usurper.

Man was designed to be the eternal associate of God Almighty, and he was formed on those lines. When he first came forth from the womb of creation, he came complete with all his faculties and forces tuned to the pitch of God's great heart-desire.

Human Dominion

God gave this wonderful being, this human, a place in His creation second only to Himself with dominion as far-reaching as Heaven and with authority over every planet and star of the Universe.

This man's voice was like the voice of God to creation.

Then man, this wonderful man, did the thing unthinkable.

He committed a crime against eternity, against his unborn progeny, against creation, against the Creator.

He committed High Treason against the Supreme Court of the Universe, against the Government of God.

He turned this love dream of God into the hands of an enemy, giving his enemy the dominion that the great Father God had given him, and it was done on such a legal basis that God could not abrogate or annul the contract.

Satan's Reign

Then began the destructive reign of Satan.

The first thing Satan did was to change the nature of the whole animal creation, and blight and blast the vegetable kingdom, and breathe into man his own diabolical nature and disposition so that the heart-treasure of God is disfigured, and man, God's man, becomes the enemy of his Father Creator.

Language is inadequate to express the horror of the first hours of the fall of man: the convulsions in the animal kingdom, the horror of Adam's awakening, the wail of distress, pain, and fear that goes up from the whole creation.

The stars even, Job tells us, were made unclean in the sight of God, the moon and the sun lost their beauty, and man, God's crown of creation, fell from his lofty estate as an under-ruler of God to a cringing, servile, lying, fearful, demon-ruled human.

The image that God had stamped upon him was slowly erased, and the image of his new father and master was penciled by Sin in its place.

So complete was man's subjection to the Devil that he turned liar the first hour, and a lie is the badge of Satanic dominion in the earth today.

Man Murders

Adam's first-born wets his hand in the blood of the second child, and Adam in the excess of his grief names his first grandchild Enosh, which means "mortal," "death-doomed," or Satan-ruled.

Creation's sorrows overflow.

Man is a spiritual bankrupt!

He has lost his approach to God; he has forfeited his legal standing; he has become a citizen of a foreign King.

He has renounced his allegiance to the great God of the Universe until he is described as "without life, without hope, without God."

When Justice makes her demand that man pay the penalty of his crime, man is unable to pay even the interest.

The penalty of man's transgression is Hell!

There was no mitigation of the sentence for the crime that man committed. It was high treason, an unpardonable sin, and this unpardonable sin of treason against God is the basic reason for the Incarnation and Substitutionary Sacrifice of God's Beloved Son.

Man had no sooner fallen under the dominion of his enemy, than the great heart of God began to plan his redemption, and so at the very gates of Eden from which man had. been driven, a sacrifice is slain and blood is spilled, and a garment of Atonement is offered to man.

Man has stripped himself and stands naked in the presence of Justice; and as you remember from a previous chapter, the word "Atonement" means a covering; so God made a covering of skins and clothes for Adam typical of Atonement for his soul which is found in the blood.

God Must Redeem

Man cannot save himself; God must provide a Redeemer.

The penalty of man's treason must be met by God if man is saved; in other words, God must assume the liabilities of man's awful treason.

If He does not, God's heart-treasure, the human, will be forever lost to Him, for man has lost his approach to God, and even his legal right to pray.

There is lying between man and God an impassable barrier like the "great gulf fixed" spoken by Jesus, where there is no bridge.

If God should assume the Liabilities of man's fall and pay man's penalty independently of man, then God will have answered the criticism of man against His Justice. In other words, if God should send His Son out of His bosom; if He should come down to the earth and become Incarnate and God should lay upon Him the entire guilt of the human race and He should go to Hell and suffer in man's stead so that no human would be obliged to suffer, then God would have vindicated Himself.

BLOOD COVENANT

Here perhaps is the most wonderful thing in the whole thought and plan of Redemption: That at the very beginning of man's peopling of the earth, God gave that which we know today as the Blood Covenant, and on the ground of this Blood Covenant every man who entered into it has the promise of a perfect redemption from all his sins.

Adam himself, the father of all the crime and sin, and heartaches and tears of the ages, had a right to this promise of a final redemption from his own guilt.

Oh, the grace and mercy of our God!

The tokens of this Covenant are extant even to this day among all primitive peoples.

We find it in Africa practiced today among all the tribes. We find it among the Bedouins and Arabs. We find it in Borneo, Tibet, China, and Japan. We find it in the Scandinavian people and among all the European nations, in Albania, Montenegro, Servia; among the Syrians, Egyptians and the Abyssinians. We find relics of it among the North American Indians, down through old Mexico, through Central America, across the Isthmus, and into South America.

In fact, the whole human race has carried traces of it down with them through all these ages, thus proving that God at the beginning made an indissoluble Covenant between Himself and the fallen human race, showing forth that in the shedding of blood of an innocent animal He would eventually give him a perfect Redemption for all his sins through the blood of His Son.

GOD ACQUITTED

God stands acquitted before the tribunal of universal human consciousness in that He did not leave man after his treason without means of salvation.

I want to call your attention to a most remarkable fact in God's dealing with the human race.

In the whole plan of Redemption we notice God's justice.

First in regard to man, God does not overlook sin nor transgression, but every sin is marked.

Second, God is just to the Devil; nowhere does God take advantage of the Devil, but God's eternal justice to frail man and to mighty Satan is manifest.

Not only is He just to man and to the Devil, but He is just to Himself.

WHAT THE CASE DEMANDS

Man's penalty for treason must be met.

That penalty is spiritual death and incarceration in Hell.

Some one must go there and pay man's penalty, for there is not a man who can represent the human race before God; neither is there a man who can stand for himself before God, for the whole human race is under indictment.

VINDICATION OF GOD FOR CREATION

God has a right to create just as a good man and a good woman have a right to give life to a child.

Adam was the master of himself, of creation, and of Satan.

Man did not have to yield unless he chose to yield.

Man was no "missing link," but He was God's crown of creation standing in the full light of perfect knowledge and dominion.

Satan was his servant and subject.

There is only one reason why Adam could have sinned.

His wife, who had yielded to the temptation, had fallen.

Adam sees the great gulf between himself and his precious wife.

THE WOMAN

We are not told that Satan visited Adam or said one word to him; all we have is the record of the conversation between Adam and his wife.

There was no ground whatever by which Adam could excuse himself.

His sin was deliberate.

It was in the face of facts.

He knew what he did and what effect it would have upon creation, upon his own children, upon his Creator God; yet for the sake of the woman, in order to regain her companionship, Adam deliberately committed high treason against God.

What a solemn warning it is to womanhood!

We know that today no nation rises above its womanhood, that few men are purer than their wife or mother.

We know that the motherhood and the wifehood of the land give us our homes.

Men may turn drunkards and debauchers and defame their marriage vows, but if the wives and mothers stand true, the home remains inviolate and children grow up clean, pure and reverent; but where the mother is a careless woman, few of her children ever stand the test of the world's temptations.

ASSUMES LIABILITIES

God must now assume the liabilities of man's transgression.

He must in some way redeem man from Satanic dominion, give back to him the forfeited life, change his nature again into harmony with His own, and defeat the Devil.

Man has lost the privilege of Sonship to God.

This Sonship privilege must be restored on legal grounds.

God cannot ignore the fact of man's hideous transgression.

That transgression must be punished, and if man is restored to God, it must be upon grounds that will not pauperize man nor rob him of his self respect; but it must be upon legal grounds that will perfectly justify man in the sight of God and give him as good a standing as though he never had sinned.

God's Justice

This work to restore man must not take advantage of Satan, because God is stronger than he. The plan that is enacted must be upon absolutely legal grounds to man, to the Devil, and to God Almighty.

Man must not only be delivered from the dominion of Satan, but there must be placed in his hands a weapon of defense and offense.

He must be given authority by which he can meet the Devil and conquer him in honorable combat; he must be able to defend himself and his children from the assaults of his old Enemy.

A resurrection of his physical body must be guaranteed and after the resurrection, Immortality, because man at the beginning had a perfect body that had power of rejuvenation.

He must be given now an eternal body over which death can have no dominion or authority.

Again, there must be a restoration of earth to the Edenic glory and beauty, and the restoration must be on such a basis that there can never be a recurrence of Satanic dominion.

Lastly, there must be legal grounds on which God can justly judge the human race and compel them to pay the penalty of sin if they reject His sin-substitute.

What God Must Do

The Redemption of man must emanate from God.

Man is a broken helpless slave without resources and in the hands of an Enemy who rules him without mercy and who has the authority to cast him into Hell.

The first thing that God must do is to provide a Redeemer.

This Redeemer must be adequate first to meet every demand of Justice; and second, every need of man; and third, He must be big enough to conquer Satan and annihilate death, and bring life and Immortality to the broken, bondaged human.

Secondly, this Redeemer must become Incarnate. That is: He as a spiritual Being must take on a human body. This human body cannot be a mortal body as ours. If it were, He would be a subject of Satan, but He must have a body patterned after the pure body of the first man, Adam.

He must be conceived and born in such a manner that He will not be a subject of Satan. He must have the same dominion and authority that the first man, Adam, had before his treason.

Third, He must be able to be a substitute for man. He must pass the examinations and requirements that Justice demands for a substitute.

He must be capable of suffering all that man would have suffered, that is, man as a whole.

He must meet the demands of Justice, and in order to do this He must go to Hell.

He must remain there under Judgment till every. demand, every legal requirement of Justice has been fully satisfied against the human race.

He must stay there and suffer until God can legally acquit every human being who takes Him as Savior and every human being who has trusted in the old Blood Covenant from the beginning.

This Redeemer cannot be an angel, nor a disembodied spirit; he cannot be any special being created for the occasion; it must be God Himself.

DEITY SUFFERS FOR MAN

Deity must suffer for humanity. The only way this can be done is for God's Beloved Son to come out of God's bosom, lay aside His glory and majesty that He has enjoyed through eternity at the Father's right hand, come down here to earth, and assume the physical body of a human.

Then God must take our sin nature, that hideous monstrous thing spiritual death, and lay it upon the Spirit of this Holy Eternal Son. The Son must go under judgment, and the wrath and indignation of Justice against sin and treason must be meted out to Him.

He must pay the wages of sin; "It is demanded" of the human, and "He becomes answerable."

After He has paid the penalty, after He has suffered till the claims of Justice are fully met, then Life Eternal must be given to His Spirit. His nature must be changed until the prophecy in the Psalms, "Thou art My son, this day have I begotten Thee," is fulfilled.

Born Out of Death

He must be born out of spiritual death into life, that Paul may say that "He is the first-born from the dead, the Head of the Church."

Then when He is Made Alive in that dark dominion of Hell, He must meet Satan, the strong, and conquer him, binding him in his own house and taking away the arms in which he is trusting; Paul graphically puts it, "He put off from Himself the principalities and the powers, and made a show of them openly, triumphing over them." This is a vivid picture of Jesus in Hell with all the hosts of demons upon Him seeking to keep Him a prisoner in their dark kingdom.

Jesus must arise in His new, omnipotent strength, hurl back the hosts of darkness and leave Satan paralyzed, as Paul tells us in Hebrews 2:14, stripped of his authority, defeated before his own mighty army.

Jesus must possess "The gate of His Enemy." He must take "The Keys of Death and Hell."

Then He must ascend up out of the darkness of Hell and enter into His body which then will be filled with light and Immortality, glorified and fitted to last through the ages of ages as the Head of the Church, and as a sample of the Resurrection.

Can Christ Meet the Demands

Will the thirty-three years of Christ's humiliation as He walked among men satisfy the claims of Justice and meet humanity's need?

You answer to the contrary.

Will the agony in the Garden of Gethsemane when He sweat great drops of blood, agony so intense that angels were obliged to come and strengthen Him before He could go on the Cross, pay the penalty of human treason?

Will the physical suffering of death on the Cross meet the penalty and set man right with God?

Was it a spiritual or a physical sin?

If the physical death of Jesus paid the penalty of man's transgression, then sin is but a physical fact.

If Jesus' physical death could pay the penalty of Sin as some contend, then why is it necessary that a Christian die?

If a Christian die physically, does he not pay the penalty of his own sin?

If physical death is the penalty for sin, then why do not the whole human race pay their own penalty and save themselves, for all die?

But we hold that the physical death of Jesus did not touch the sin issue at all; it was only a means to an end, and the real suffering of Jesus, the Substitute, must be spiritual as well as physical.

Can God demand spiritual suffering from the human race, that is, suffering in Hell, if His Substitute only suffered physically?

Can God justly send the human race to Hell, and finally into the Lake of Fire, the great Federal Prison of Eternity, unless His Son went to Hell and suffered there for the human race?

But some will say that annihilation is the penalty of sin, and that the sinner when he dies is annihilated.

Well, if this be true, and if Jesus is our sin Substitute, then He must have been annihilated; and, as one has said in this connection, if "Jesus must have been annihilated," then who was it that was raised from the dead?

There would have been a break in the continuity of personality, and the one who was annihilated could not have been raised from the dead for he would have ceased to be, and another being would have had to have been created to appear as the Christ.

This argument falls by its own folly.

This Redeemer must experience death for every man, so that every man may have a legal right to eternal life and Sonship with God.

If He goes to Hell and suffers for the human race, then God stands vindicated and man is silent. Man no longer has a case against God for He has sent out of Heaven His own Son who has come to the earth and has paid the penalty of man's guilt without asking man to have any part in the awful transaction.

If He did not go to Hell and suffer, God cannot send any man to Hell who rejects Him as a Savior; but if He did go to Hell, then God has not only a legal right to send every man to Hell that rejects Him, but God must send him there in order to be just towards Jesus the Substitute.

If God can save one human being who rejects Jesus Christ as a personal Savior, then God could save the whole human race, because there is no distinction.

All are spiritually dead, all are subject of Satan, and if one could have been saved, then the whole world could have been saved.

If the whole could have been saved apart from Christ, then God's sending Jesus to Hell is the most colossal crime ever committed in the Universe.

Man's transgression is but child's play in comparison to the unspeakable crime of sending the Holy, innocent Son of God into Hell's dark recesses as our sin Substitute, if it were not necessary.

If this be true, then every man who rejects Jesus must legally go to Hell regardless of God's feelings, and every man that accepts Jesus must legally go to Heaven.

This gives God a right to sit as Judge on the great White Throne and it seals man's lips forever.

‡ ‡ ‡

Questions

1. Why must God, Himself, provide man's redeemer?
2. What was the purpose of the Blood Covenant which God gave to man after he sinned?
3. What must God do in order to be just toward man, Satan, and Himself?
4. How has God vindicated Himself of all charges of unrighteousness that man could bring against Him?
5. Give the steps the Christ must take in order to redeem man.

"Surely He hath borne our diseases and carried our pains: yet we did esteem him stricken, smitten of God, and afflicted. But he was wounded for our transgressions___ he was bruised for our iniquities; the chastisement of our peace was upon Him: and with His stripes we are healed. All we like sheep have gone astray; we have turned everyone to his own way; and Jehovah hath laid upon him the iniquity of us all." Isa. 53:4-6.

"Yet now hath he reconciled in the body of his flesh through death, to present you holy and without blemish and unreprovable before him." Col. 1:22.

"Him who knew no sin He made to be sin on our behalf; that we might become the righteousness of God in Him." 2 Cor. 5:21.

"But he when he had offered one sacrifice for sins forever, sat down on the right hand of God — For by one offering he hath perfected forever them that are sanctified." Heb. 10:12-14.

Chapter The Ninth

THE SIN BEARER

OD began to speak through the Prophets as soon as man fell, promising that a Redeemer should come who would break the dominion of Satan and restore to man his lost dominion and standing.

In Isaiah 7:14, we have a declarative statement of the Incarnation.

The first step in man's Redemption must be the Incarnation of Deity, or, to use our own language, the union of God and man.

"Therefore the Lord Himself shall give you a sign; behold the virgin shall conceive, and bear a Son, and shall call his name Immanuel."

It is a striking sentence, "The Lord Himself."

The Hebrew word "Adonai" means literally the Ruling One, the God of Miracles, of wonders, of Majesty; and notice he says, "The Lord Himself," emphasizing His might and power, "shall give you a sign" or miraculous work and wonder for your special benefit.

"Behold the Virgin," as though looking down through the ages, He marks her out.

She is to be a daughter of the House of David, and she shall conceive and bear a Son.

Mark you, it is to be a Virgin, a woman who has never known a man, who shall bear a Son, and His name, and here we are thrilled, shall be called "Immanuel," that is, God with us, or more literally, Incarnation.

This child shall be called Immanuel or Incarnation, wonderful name.

Here God suggests the union of Deity and humanity.

Notice then first, that He is to be of the House of David; second, "the Lord Himself shall give a sign," something supernatural, a miracle is going to be performed; third, the Virgin is the God-assigned one; and fourth, He is to be a Son, a male; and fifth, His name is Incarnation.

Isaiah 9:6-7, "For unto us a Child is born, unto us a Son is given; the Government shall be upon His shoulders, and His name shall be called Wonderful, Counsellor, Mighty God, Everlasting Father, Prince of Peace."

Here the Prophet says, "Unto us," a national Child, "A son is given," Israel's Son, a national Son.

"The Government shall be upon His shoulders," He shall come as a Ruler to have authority and dominion.

Had we space I would like to show you that from Genesis 3 through the entire prophetical utterances concerning the Coming One there is always a double prophecy; one we might call the bass in the great oratorio of Redemption, the Lordship and dominion of the Coming One.

He is going to break the Dominion of Satan; He is going to set men free.

He is going to bruise the head of the Serpent; He is going to grind him under His heel.

But His name here is perhaps the most striking: "Wonderful Counsellor," the great Lawyer of God's family; second, "Mighty God"; no Jewish mother would have dared to call her child that, for it would have been the rankest blasphemy, and she and her child both would have been subject to stoning; third, "Everlasting Father," indicating that this wonderful Being is going to be a Revealer of the Father, which we find Him in the Gospel of John; and lastly, He is called by that beautiful name, "Prince of Peace."

Turn with me to the Gospel of Luke and read the sweetest story ever penned, of the conception of the Son of God.

Luke 1:26-38, "Now in the sixth month the angel Gabriel was sent from God unto a city of Galilee, named Nazareth, to a virgin betrothed to a man whose name was Joseph, of the house of David; and the virgin's name was Mary.

"And he came unto her, and said, Hail, thou that art highly favored, the Lord is with thee.

"But she was greatly troubled at the saying, and cast in her mind what manner of salutation this might be.

"And the angel said unto her, Fear not, Mary: for thou hast found favor with God.

"And behold, thou shalt conceive in thy womb, and bring forth a son, and shalt call his name Jesus.

"He shall be great, and shall be called the Son of the Most High: and the Lord God shall give unto Him the throne of His father David: and He shall reign over the house of Jacob forever; and of His kingdom there shall be no end.

"And Mary said unto the angel, How shall this be, seeing I know not a man?

"And the angel answered and said unto her, The Holy Spirit shall come upon thee, and the power of the Most High shall overshadow thee: wherefore also the holy thing which is begotten shall be called the Son of God.

"And behold, Elizabeth thy kinswoman, she also hath conceived a son in her old age; and this is the sixth month with her that was called barren.

"For no word from God shall be void of power. "And Mary said, Behold, the handmaid of the Lord; be it unto me according to thy word.

"And the angel departed from her."

John 1:14, "And the Word became flesh, and dwelt among us (and we beheld His glory, glory as of the only begotten from the Father), full of grace and truth."

Here we have the story told of the union of Deity and humanity: a child conceived in a virgin's womb by supernatural manifestations of the Creator of the human, because man, by his apostasy and awful sin, had necessitated a second miracle, greater than the miracle of creation, to encompass his Redemption from the power and guilt of his own transgressions.

In Matthew 3:17, when Jesus was baptized, we hear the Father say, "This is My beloved son, in whom I am well pleased."

By this we know that Jesus perfectly pleased the Father during His earth walk, and all through the Gospel of John we discover Him as the Father-pleaser.

He says of Himself, "I came not to do my own will, but the will of Him that sent me; I seek not my own will but the will of Him whose work I came to accomplish."

And again, "I do always the things that are pleasing to Him," revealing to us a sample Son, seeking only His Father's will, the first man since the Fall who made it His business to do the will of the great Father God.

In Luke 4, we have the graphic picture of the temptation of Jesus.

Here He faces Satan as Adam faced him in the Garden of Eden, but unlike the first Man He conquers Satan.

He faces the long forty days of hunger. He faces the desire to reach the human race and save it by another road than the cross and Hell, but He puts it far from Him.

He turns with joy to walk with His Mighty Father, and in Isaiah we come to the great picture of the Substitutionary sacrifice of the Lamb of God. ·

This picture that I want to give you is the divine side of the Crucifixion.

Turn for a few moments and read the story of the Crucifixion from Mark or Luke. There you see that strange Galilean arrested first in the Garden of Gethsemane, taken down to the Hall of Caiaphas the High Priest, then blindfolded and spit upon, insulted and struck in the presence of the very High Priest of God, and then you witness the long, long, cold, weary hours until He is taken before Pilate and then eventually to Herod to be mocked and jeered, to be clothed with the mock garment of kingly authority and with a mock crown of thorns upon His brow, and the mock badge of kingly authority within His hand, and then the long weary march back to Pilate, and the trial, proceeding with bitterness and jealousy. You find Him standing calm and quiet with no part in this unnatural scene, except that of the innocent victim of jealousy and hate.

We see Him scourged, His back laid open by the awful Roman lictor.

Blood flows, and flesh is torn as the cruel blows fall mercilessly upon His bared back.

Then His clothes are thrown roughly about Him, and He is started out for Golgotha, staggering beneath His own Cross. We see Him fall under its weight, and Simon of Cyrene is compelled to bear it. Then we see Him staggering blindly up the mountain side, surrounded by the soldiery, and finally reaching the crest. A circle is formed. He is laid roughly down upon the Cross on His back, and the Roman soldiers with cruel hate drive the spikes into His hands and feet; then He is lifted up naked, and the Cross is dropped into the socket in the rock.

Jesus the Nazarene is crucified!

We watch the mob as it surges backward and forward about the Cross.

We hear the High Priest hurling his bitter taunts in the face of the suffering Galilean.

We hear the mob in their bitter denunciation, led on by their great Priesthood.

It was a sight not for angels, nor for men, but for demons only.

But the vision I want you to have is not of the physical suffering of Jesus, not what man has done as that is only a means to an end, but come behind the scenes and see the agony of the Son of God, and see Him smitten by His own God, His own Father.

Peter tells us on the day of Pentecost that He was delivered up by the determinate counsel and the foreknowledge of God.

Now I think we can understand this wonderful prophecy, "Surely He hath borne our diseases and carried our pains, yet we did esteem Him stricken, smitten of God and afflicted."

In the Four Gospels we see Him only stricken of man, but the Prophet sees Him as He hangs there, the outcast of men, "stricken, smitten of God, and afflicted."

God is dealing with our sin Substitute; He is dealing not with His body but with His soul and spirit.

"He was wounded for our transgressions. He was bruised for our iniquities; the chastisement of our peace was upon Him, and with His stripes we are healed. All we like sheep have gone astray; we have turned every one to his own way, and Jehovah made to strike upon Him the iniquity of us all."

Here we see God taking our sin nature, hideous spiritual death, and making it to strike, as the Prophet says, upon His soul.

"Him who knew no sin," God is now making to be sin.

He who has basked in the presence of His Father, He who has so charmed the very heart of His Great Father God as a Man until He cried out, "This is My beloved Son in whom I am well pleased," is now man's sin substitute.

He has taken Man's place, and the whole human race is now represented in Him, and as He hangs there under judgment on the accursed tree, God takes your sin and mine, yes, the sin of the whole world and lets it fall upon the sensitive spirit until the sin of a world has entered into His very Being and He has become the outcast from Heaven, until God turns His back upon Him, and He cries out, "My God, My God, why hast Thou forsaken Me."

"By oppression and judgment, He was taken away" or literally, "it was demanded and He became answerable."

"And as for His generation, who among them considered that He was cut off from the land of the living for the transgression of my people to whom the stroke was due."

Literally, He was cut out of the realm of life and went into the realm of death for His people to whom the stroke was due.

"And He made His grave with the wicked and with a rich man in His death."

This word "Death" is in the plural in the original.

It is a very remarkable fact that this is the only time that the word "deaths" is used in the entire Old Testament Scriptures, except when it speaks of Satan's being cast out of Heaven, that he "died the deaths."

It is used here, because the Prophet saw that our sin Substitute when He went on the Cross died spiritually as well as physically; so it says "in His deaths."

"Yet it pleased Jehovah to bruise Him; He hath put Him to grief; when thou shalt make His soul an offering for sin . . . He shall see the travail of His soul and shall be satisfied."

Notice that it is not the physical suffering of Jesus, but His soul travail; God has made His soul an offering for sin.

God has laid upon Him the iniquity of us all, and God is watching the travail, the deep agony, the birth-throes of the Son of God.

It is out of this birth-travail that the church is born.

"And on the ground of this shall My Righteous Servant legally acquit many, because He shall bear their transgressions." This is a Literal Translation of Isa. 53.

This picture of the fierce sufferings of Jesus finds a parallel in the 88th Psalm.

Here we have a view of Christ in Hell actually bearing our sins, suffering in our stead, cast off by God, in utter despair, suffering what we should have suffered.

This 88th Psalm is the story of a righteous man in Hell, undergoing the most hideous pain and suffering.

It cannot belong to any other individual than our sin Substitute; the whole language is Messianic.

"For my soul is full of troubles, and my life draweth nigh unto Sheol.

"I am reckoned with them that go down into the pit; I am as a man that hath no help, cast off among the dead, like the slain that lie in the grave, whom thou rememberest no more, and they are cut off from thy hand.

"Thou hast laid me in the lowest pit, in dark places, in the deeps.

"Thy wrath lieth hard upon me, and thou hast afflicted me with all thy waves.

"Thou hast put mine acquaintance far from me; thou hast made me an abomination unto them: I am shut up, and I cannot come forth.

"Mine eye wasteth away by reason of affliction: I have daily called upon thee, O Jehovah; I have spread forth my hands unto thee.

"Wilt thou show wonders to the dead?

"Shall they that are deceased arise and praise thee?

"Shall thy loving kindness be declared in the grave, or thy faithfulness in Destruction?

"Shall thy wonders be known in the dark, and thy righteousness in the land of forgetfulness?

"But unto thee, O Jehovah, have I cried: and in the morning shall my prayer come before thee.

"Jehovah, why castest thou off my soul?

"Why hidest thou thy face from me?

"I am afflicted and ready to die from my youth up: While I suffer thy terrors I am distracted.

"Thy fierce wrath is gone over me; thy terrors have cut me off.

"They came round me like water all the day long: they compassed me about together."

In the third verse he says, "My life draweth nigh unto Sheol," unto Hell, the place of torment, "I am reckoned with them that go down into the pit," "cast off among the dead like the slain that lie in the grave, whom thou rememberest no more; thou hast laid me in the lowest pit, in dark places, in the deeps."

Here He has gone to the very depths of agony in suffering for man; He is laid in the lowest Hell.

"Thy wrath lieth hard upon me; thou hast afflicted me with all thy waves."

None but He ever had all the wrath of God laid upon him.

He is the only one whom this prophecy could mean.

"I am shut up, I cannot come forth, and then He cries, "Wilt thou show wonders to the dead? Shall they that are deceased rise and praise thee? Shall thy loving kindness be declared in the grave, or thy faithfulness in destruction? Shall thy wonders be known in the dark, and thy righteousness in the land of forgetfulness?"

Here the four outstanding attributes of Deity are mentioned: loving kindness, faithfulness, omnipotence, and righteousness.

These are the four prominent attributes of the Throne of God, and the writer says, "Shall these four great attributes of God be shown in the depths of Hell."

What can he mean?

Just this, that when Jesus Christ, our sin Substitute, went down into Hell, there He proclaimed God's loving kindness to the wicked human race.

There demons and men were compelled to say,

"Behold, how God must love man to send His own Son out of His own bosom into this dread place to suffer on our account."

Man had challenged God's love down there in Hades.

He challenged it in the Garden of Eden.

He has at every epoch of history.

But now God puts it beyond doubt, for while we were yet sinners, Christ goes down into the dark regions of the damned to suffer in our stead.

The eternal faithfulness of God is shown in Hell: God has been faithful to His promises.

If God were ever going to fail in any place, He surely would have failed here when it came to the issue of sending His Son down there for our sins, but He kept His covenant with Abraham.

He kept His word with David, and down in Hell the heralds of the damned were obliged to cry out, "Behold the loving kindness and the eternal faithfulness of the Great God of the Universe."

His omnipotence, His awful power, power that could speak the Universe into being with a word, was declared in Hell when Jesus Christ, after having suffered the demands of Justice, arose in His might and conquered Satan and left him paralyzed and broken on the very pavements of Hell, in the presence of a defeated and fear-stricken host.

"And thy righteousness in the land of forgetfulness?" God's righteousness, the foundation of His Throne, who can ever challenge it again?

He that denuded Heaven of its light, glory, and joy, He that insisted that His Son not only go on the Cross but into Hell itself to pay the penalty of Man's high treason, He that is omnipotent but would not take advantage of Satan after he had won his conquest over man, although He could have by one word wiped the human race from the earth, yet suffered them to go on until He could assume the liabilities of their awful guilt and pay man's penalty, cannot again be accused of injustice.

God was just to man, and He was just to Satan.

God would not ask man to stand in His presence through Eternity until every whit of guilt and every charge had been wiped off the books and man stood as clean and as free as though sin had never pierced his soul.

God would not pardon man until an adequate sacrifice had been made.

And so in Hell Jesus Christ proclaims the love of God, the won-der-working omnipotence of God and the eternal righteousness of God. When the great White Throne Judgment comes and the hosts of demons and men come to stand before that great Tribunal, those who were then in Hell will come and in the presence of that awful multitude will answer to God's justice that was declared in Hell.

Every demon, every human will know that God was just.

There is no doubt but that in the Archives of Hell a record has been kept of the visit of the Eternal Son when He went there as man's Substitute under judgment, under the awful burden of the guilt of man's sin.

What He suffered, none of us can know.

Holy, as God was Holy, pure, as God was pure, yet for you and for me that precious Being sank to the lowest depths of Hell.

"Thou hast laid me in the lowest depths, all thy wrath is upon me"; He cries in His bitterness, "Jehovah, why casteth thou off my soul, why hidest thou thy face from me?"

We see Him hanging on the Cross, He cries, "My God, my God, why hast Thou forsaken Me?"

Forsaken by the Father, forsaken by the angels who had min-istered unto Him through Eternity, He feels the waves sweep around the Cross and the darkness of the lower depths come up and sweep over the earth and obscure the light of the sun.

Oh, that awful hour when the cry of the Substitute rent the sky!

> I stood one night, on Calv'ry's height,
>   Where hung the Son of man;
> I raised mine eyes to starry skies,
>   Mused on redemption's plan.
> I saw the fall, sin's bitter thrall,
>   Where plunged the human race!
> I heard the moan that thrilled the throne,
>   And moved the God of grace.

I saw the Son, the Spotless One,
  Come from His Father's side;
In form prepared, our nature shared,
  And for the sinner died.
I saw the tree, He died for me,
  Forsaken by His God;
I saw the blood, the crimson flood
  Dripping upon the sod.

I heard His cry, that pierced the sky,
  The sad wail of the lost;
My God, My God, He's kissed the rod,
  And pain sin's awful cost.
I heard the wail, as men turned pale,
  The earth reeled at the stroke. .
Sin's work was done, it slew the Son,
  Its billows o'er Him broke.

His soul travail doth now prevail,
  Man's penalty is borne;
Hell feels His might, yields Him the fight
  On resurrection morn.
I heard Him say: "Go, tell today
  The good news to the race;
By God's decree, all men are free,
  Saved by the Father's grace."

In Matthew 12:40 Jesus declares that as Jonah was three days and three nights in the fish's belly, so shall the son of man be three days and three nights in the heart of the earth.

In Peter's sermon on the day of Pentecost, Acts 2:22-34, that sample sermon of the church, this awful truth of the substitutionary sacrifice of Jesus is clearly set forth.

"Ye men of Israel, hear these words: Jesus of Nazareth, a man approved of God unto you by mighty works and wonders and signs which God did by Him in the midst of you, even as ye yourselves know; Him, being delivered up by the determinate counsel and foreknowledge of God, ye by the hand of lawless men did crucify and slay: Whom God raised up, having loosed the pangs of death: because it was not possible that He should be holden of it.

"For David said concerning him . . . Because thou wilt not leave my soul unto Hades, neither wilt thou give thy Holy One to see corruption . . .

"Brethren, I may say unto you freely of the patriarch David, that he both died and was buried, and his tomb is with us unto this day.

"Being therefore a prophet, and knowing that God has sworn with an oath to him, that of the fruit of his loins he would set one upon his throne; he foreseeing this spake of the resurrection of the Christ, that neither was he left unto Hades, nor did his flesh see corruption.

"This Jesus did God raise up, whereof we are all witnesses.

"Being therefore by the right hand of God exalted, and having received of the Father the promise of the Holy Spirit, he hath poured forth this, which ye see and hear."

24th verse, "Whom God raised up having loosed the pangs of death, because it was not possible for Him to be holden of it."

Notice this, that when Jesus was raised from the dead He was loosed out of birth pangs.

The Greek word for birth pangs literally means birth throes, birth agonies, which is stronger than travail or our English word "pangs."

When Jesus was raised from the Dead, He was loosed out of that kind of suffering, agony beyond expression.

The 27th verse, "Because thou wilt not leave my soul unto Hades, neither shall thy Holy one see corruption," notice that His soul was not going to be left in Hades, neither was His body to suffer corruption in Joseph's tomb.

Peter waxes eloquent and says, "He foreseeing this spake of the resurrection of Christ, that neither was He left in Hades, nor did His flesh see corruption."

Peter believed that Jesus went to Hell and that during the three days and three nights, He suffered the unspeakable agonies of torture, and that when He was raised from the dead, He was raised out of birth agony and suffering. It was out of these birth agonies that the Church was born.

Romans 10:6-7, "Say not in thy heart, Who shall ascend into Heaven? (that is, to bring Christ down;) or, Who shall descend into (the Bottomless Pit) the Abyss? (that is, to bring Christ up from the dead") or more literally, "from among the dead."

Here Paul makes the allusion to the well known fact, the basis of his entire teaching of the Substitutionary Sacrifice, that Jesus went down into the Abyss of Hell, in suffering for man.

He speaks of the same thing in Ephesians 4:9-10, "Now this, He ascended, what is it but that He also descended into the lowest parts of the earth? He that descended is the same also that ascended far above all the heavens."

In 1 Peter 3:18 (Rotherham), "Because Christ also once for all concerning sins died, just in behalf of the unjust, in order that He might introduce us to God, being put to death indeed in flesh but made alive in spirit."

You notice in this, that He was made alive in spirit; He would not have been made alive in spirit had not He died in spirit.

You remember, I called your attention to the fact that Jesus died in spirit on the Cross, before He died in the flesh.

In all these references in Romans where it speaks of Christ's dying, in every case it has reference to a spiritual instead of a physical death.

Here it declares that Jesus not only died in the flesh, physically, but that He also died in spirit, spiritually, and therefore His resurrection was a double resurrection.

He was made alive, first in spirit, and then in the flesh.

1 Timothy 3:16 tells us that He was justified in spirit, that is, He died under Judgment, condemned, and before He arose from the dead, God legally justified Him in spirit.

In Colossians 2:15 it speaks of His resurrection and tells us that, "He put off from Himself the principalities and the powers, and made a show of them openly, triumphing over them in it."

Here is a picture of Christ in Hell, with the whole host of demons attempting to keep Him there, but when the penalty of our sin had been fully met, Satan had no power to hold Him longer.

Paul tells us, that "He was delivered up, on account of our trespasses, and was raised when we stood right with God."

The very moment the sin problem was settled, that moment Jesus Christ was legally justified, was made alive in spirit once more, and assumed His wonderful dominion, authority, and power. Hurling back the hosts of demons, He became the Master of Hell; putting them off from Himself, He hurled them hopeless and powerless back into the dark abyss.

Jesus, the Conqueror

No wonder the angel said, "Ye seek Jesus who was crucified? Come see the place where the Lord lay."

He died as Jesus our Substitute, the Lamb that beareth away the sin of the world.

He arose as Lord, as Master of death, of Hell and of the grave.

Hear Him cry to John, "I was dead and behold I am alive for evermore, and I have the keys of death and of Hades."

The matchless, mighty Christ had gone into the strong room, the very citadel of Hell, into the crown room of the Black Prince and Ruler of death; He had conquered him in honorable combat; He had taken from him his authority, his dominion; He brings it back and offers it to fallen man through His matchless name and grace.

O Christ, what agonies, what wounds for man hast Thou borne.

Our feeble minds cannot grasp the meaning of these awful words, but our spirit knows, Great Christ, that Thou hast redeeemed us from death and from Hell.

What does this mean to us?

It means that every man who takes Jesus Christ as his Savior and confesses Him as his Lord, stands legally acquitted in the presence of God.

It means that God is vindicated: He can now save the Believers and judge the sinners.

Satan is defeated, and man can be free.

Man is legally justified, heir to eternal life and Sonship privileges.

Heaven is legally the home of God's children.

Hell is legally the home of sinners.

ADDITIONAL FACTS ABOUT THE SIN-BEARER

"Behold the Lamb of God that beareth away the sin of the world," John 1:29.

Jesus is our sin-bearer.

When did Jesus bear our sins?

According to some teachers He bore them from all eternity, basing the theory upon that faulty rendering of Rev. 13:8 when it should read this way, "And all that dwell upon the earth shall worship Him, every one whose name hath not been written from the foundation of the world in the Book of Life of the Lamb that hath been slain."

Instead of the Lamb's being slain from the foundation of the world, it really says that our names are written in the Book of Life from the foundation of the world.

Our Savior did not bear sin for us as a substitute until He went on the Cross.

He evidently hung on the Cross three hours before He became our sin-bearer.

He became the sin-bearer the moment that God took our sins and laid them upon His spirit; then His whole spirit underwent a change, and He passed under the dominion of spiritual death and Satan.

It was then that He cried out, "My God, my God, why hast Thou forsaken me?" Now the blighting curse of our sins is upon Him. He is now shut out from the presence of God, His own Father, as our sin-bearer. For hours He hangs there until finally He cried, "It is finished," and yields up His Spirit.

He does not mean that His substitutionary work is finished, for that could not be until He rose from the dead and carried the tokens of His victory into Heaven's Holy of Holies, laying them down before the Father. It did mean that as a man, and a Jew, He had fulfilled the Mosaic Law; that He had satisfied the heart-claims of the Father God as a Son, and that He had done everything that was necessary for our redemption as a perfect man.

Now He must go into the dreaded regions and pay the penalty of our sinful nature.

Some have thought that the great suffering in Gethsemane was due to the fact that God was laying sin upon Him then; others have said it was a struggle with the devil who was trying to slay Him. All these are beside the issue.

Jno. 10:18. Neither angels nor demons could slay Jesus until He had become mortal, and He did not become mortal until our sin was laid upon Him and He had died spiritually.

Again, there was no sin on Jesus in Gethsemane. He was well-pleasing to the Father. The Beloved Son was strengthened by Angels there, but when He hung on the Cross there was no angelic ministration. He suffered alone, an outcast from God and a substitute for the whole world.

The real suffering of Gethsemane was this: He saw that as a sin-substitute He must be separated from His Father and must become a subject of Satan, and more than that, that He must become sin.

He, who was as Holy as God is Holy, He in whom sin had never found place, must now become the accursed one. His whole Being shrank from it, and He cried out, "Father if it be possible take this cup from me," and in His awful agony and struggle He continued, "Not my will but Thine be accomplished."

It was not the cry of submission; it was the cry of the Hero Christ, the Hero Man, our princely Saviour God.

He would go through Hell itself for our redemption.

A Further Word on Jesus' Dual Death

Isaiah 53:9. "They made His grave with the wicked and with a rich man in His death (Heb. Deaths): although He had done no violence, neither was any deceit in His mouth."

The nature of the Death of Jesus holds the key to His Substitutionary Sacrifice.

Was it merely Physical, or was there a Spiritual Death, a Death of His spirit?

This quotation from Isaiah gives us a key; it declares, "They made His grave with a rich man in His deaths."

Man was spiritually dead and in order to pay the penalty of Man's transgression Christ must, as Paul tells us in Heb. 2:9, "Experience death for every man."

We know that the Physical Death of Jesus would not satisfy the claims of Justice; so it was necessary that He become identified with our union with the devil, that He actually die spiritually and become a partaker of Spiritual Death.

If He did this, then He could be sent to the same place that we should have to be sent for our guilt.

The fact of His Dual Death is brought out very clearly in the New Testament.

In Paul's sermon in Acts 13:32-34 Paul says, "And we bring you good tidings of the promise made unto the fathers, that God hath fulfilled the same unto our children, in that he raised up Jesus; as also it is written in the second psalm, Thou art my Son, this day have I begotten Thee. And as concerning that He raised Him up from the dead, now no more to return to corruption."

He is speaking here of the Resurrection of the Lord Jesus, and he says that when Jesus was raised from the dead that He was begotten of the Father.

In other words, He was born of the Spirit.

What does he mean by it?

It has no reference whatever to Jesus' birth as a Babe in the Manger in Bethlehem.

It has reference to His Resurrection.

We know that when Jesus died it was under the curse, and that God had laid our sin upon Him. Him who knew no sin, God had made to become sin on our behalf.

We know that He was reckoned among them that are cast off.

We know that as Moses lifted up the Serpent in the wilderness Jesus was also lifted up a serpent; that is, He was a partaker of Satanic Nature, the old Serpent.

He was a partaker of our nature when this happened, when God laid our sin nature upon Him while on the cross.

Peter tells us, "Christ also suffered for sin, once, the Righteous for the unrighteous that He might bring us to God being put to death in the flesh but made alive in the spirit."

There is no article before the word flesh and spirit in the Greek, and it should read "being put to death in flesh but made alive in spirit."

Now when was Jesus made alive in spirit?

That does not mean the Holy Spirit, that means His own spirit, Himself.

It was at the Resurrection; of course, He could not have been made alive unless He was dead.

Now we understand what Paul means in Heb. 2:9 "that He experienced death for every man."

In 1 Timothy 3:16 Paul tells us that He was justified in spirit.

He could not be Justified until He was first condemned, and we know that He was not Justified until the claims of Justice had been fully satisfied; then the edict comes from the Throne of God, and our Substitute stands legally acquitted in the presence of the demons in Hell.

Next He is given Eternal Life, and He that was Spiritually dead and under Satan's Dominion is now made alive in spirit. God says, "Thou art My Son, this day have I begotten Thee."

In Col. 1:18, "And He is the head of the body, the church: who is the beginning, the first born from the dead; that in all things He might have the pre-eminence."

GRACE BASED UPON RIGHTEOUSNESS

"That as sin reigned in death, even so might grace reign through righteousness unto Eternal Life through Jesus Christ our Lord."

Sin reigned in the realm of death: Grace reigns in the realm of life, but Grace reigns on the basis of Justice.

When God extended grace to us in Jesus Christ, He did it on the ground of Justice.

If His love has operated in the Sacrifice of Christ for the human race, that love has been based upon Justice.

God did not offer remission of sins, or Eternal Life, or the benefits of Sonship to the human until He had a legal right to do it.

Justice is the foundation of the Throne of God.

God would not offer the sinner remission and Sonship, regardless of His love for him, until He could do it justly, for if He did He would pauperize the man who accepted it.

Therfore, it was necessary before love could operate that the claims of Justice be satisfied, so God sent His Son down there to pay humanity's claims to Justice, and when He had perfectly satisfied the claims of Justice, love was permitted to reach her hand out to the human.

Had God pardoned a sinner and given him Sonship rights before the claims of Justice against man had been satisfied, God would have been unjust, but He did not do this.

God has always in all His dealings operated upon the ground of perfect Justice. Therefore, when a sinner accepts Jesus Christ on the ground of Grace, he is doing it on Grace that is founded in Justice.

When God makes a present to man, He has a right to make the present.

He has taken advantage of no one.

His gift is as free as perfect Justice could make it.

This gives a dignity and beauty to Christianity that no other religion has.

It gives a sense of manliness and virility to Christianity that it could not have if God had in any wise allowed Love to usurp the place of Justice; but when Justice is laid as a foundation, Love has a right to build thereon.

‡   ‡   ‡

Questions

1. Explain fully Isaiah 7:14.

2. In what scripture do we have the story told of the union of Deity and humanity?

3. Explain fully Christ's dual death.

4. Why is it that Christ's physical death would not have met the claims of Justice?

5. Explain Christ's being made alive out of spiritual death and His conquering Satan.

Eternal life is the nature of God that is imparted to man at the new birth, making him a New Creation. Man's need of Eternal Life was the reason for Redemption.

"I came that they may have life and may have it abundantly." Jn. 10:10.

"Even as thou gavest Him authority over all whom thou hast given Him that He should give Eternal Life, and this is life eternal that they should know thee the only true God, and Him whom thou didst send, even Jesus Christ." Jn. 17:2, 3.

"Verily, verily, I say unto you, He that heareth my word, and believeth him that sent me hath Eternal Life, and cometh not unto judgment, but hath passed out of death into life." — "For as the Father hath life in Himself even so gave He to the son also to have life in Himself." Jn. 5:24, 26.

"Whereby He hath granted unto us His precious and exceeding great promises; that through these ye may become partakers of the Divine nature." 2 Peter 1:4.

Chapter The Tenth

ETERNAL LIFE

NE day a Jewish lawyer came to Jesus and said, "Good Master, what shall I do to inherit Eternal Life?"

This young man represented the most zealous branch of the family of Abraham, children of the promise and of the Covenant; yet he knew that he did not have the one thing above all other things that made him right with God.

On the great day of Atonement when his sins were forgiven, he went away conscious of the fact that the real thing had not been made right in his life.

The hunger was still unsatisfied, the craving, unmet.

He wanted, he needed, he felt the lack of something in his nature that seemed to have been lost somewhere, sometime not from his nature alone but from the nature of the human.

It was something that he knew would round out and complete his joy and longings.

What was it?

It was something greater than Atonement, greater than Justification under the law, greater than mere Forgiveness.

The thing he craved is majored in the Gospel of John — it is a single word.

This word is the key to the gospel of John: it is the key that unlocks the divine side of the plan of redemption.

It is the biggest word of the Gospel.

It is the word that stands for the whole heart-teaching of the Gospel of the Grace of God — it is the word "Life." Eternal Life — the Nature of God.

Man is spiritually dead.

Spiritual death, as you noticed in the previous chapter, is the nature of the Devil that was imparted to man at the Fall.

It is the eradication of this Devil nature that God has been working for in all the ages.

This was the reason for Jesus' Coming to the earth.

The only thing that will reach man's need is the nature of God, Eternal Life.

Nothing can take its place.

It is the one imperative need that lifts its voice above all the other needs of the human.

Christianity is supernatural.

It was foreshadowed by a supernatural Judaism.

It culminates in Jesus, the supernatural man, who was supernatural in His birth, in His life, in His death, in His resurrection, in His ascension, in the gift of the Holy Spirit on the day of Pentecost, in the birth of the Church on that great day, and in the rebirth of every child of God.

Here is where Christianity differs from every other religion.

A Christian is one who has received Eternal Life, the nature of God.

This is that divine act that changes a man from the Family of Satan to the Family of God instantaneously.

Man is naturally an enemy of God.

God imparts to him His own nature; this instantly changes man's being and spirit.

It may be interesting for us to notice the nature of Eternal Life.

John 5:26, "For as the Father hath life in Himself even so gave He to the Son also to have life in Himself."

Eternal Life is the nature of God.

It is the Being, the Substance of God.

In 2 Peter 1:4, we are told that we "become partakers of the divine nature, having escaped from the corruption that is in the world through lust."

The corruption from which we escaped is spiritual death, the Satanic nature.

Here he declares that we become partakers of the Divine nature.

We read in Eph. 2:1, "You hath He made alive when ye were dead in your trespasses and sins," and John 5:24, "He that heareth my word, and believeth him that sent me, hath Eternal life, and cometh not into judgment, but hath passed out of death into life."

And John also tells us in 1 John 3:14, "We know that we have passed out of death into life, because we love the brethren."

From these Scriptures, we see that Eternal Life is the nature of God, that to become a child of God means that we become partakers of the Divine Nature, Eternal Life.

When this takes place we pass out of death, the realm of Satan, into Life, the realm of God, out of the dominion of Satan into the dominion of Christ, the Lord and head of the church.

When we receive Eternal Life, Satanic nature passes out of us, not theoretically but actually, and we that were dead are made alive. Col. 1:13-14.

Paul states it clearly in 2 Cor. 5:17. "Wherefore if any man be in Christ, he is a new creature, the old things are passed away; behold they are become new, all things are of God."

Literally, if any man be in Christ there is a new creature, or a new creation, something that has just been spoken into existence, as a new star, a full grown tree, a house that had never been before. So it reads, "Wherefore if any man be in Christ, there is a new creation," not a modified creation, not a fixed-over creation, but a new creation.

Spiritual death gave to man physical death, or mortality, for his body.

The new birth gives Eternal Life to the spirit of man, and the promise of Immortality for our physical bodies at the return of our Lord Jesus.

How Eternal Life Is Available

Let us read first that great Scripture in the Gospel of John, 20:30-31, "Many other signs therefore did Jesus in the presence of the disciples, which are not written in this book; but these are written, that ye may believe that Jesus is the Christ, the Son of God; and that believing, ye may have life in His name."

Notice how John puts it here. Jesus did a great many things and said a great many things that are not recorded in this book, but he recorded these things for this purpose, "that ye might believe that Jesus is the Christ, the Son of God, and that believing ye might have Life in His name."

The object, then, is that we may have Eternal Life.

The first step is to read what is written in the Gospels that we may know that Jesus is the Son of God. For if He is the Son of God — then He has made Eternal Life available to spiritually dead man.

1 Cor. 15:3-4. For until we know this, seeking Eternal Life will be in vain, but having satisfied our intellects that Jesus is the Son of God, that He died for our sins according to the Scripture, and that He arose again according to Scripture, we can take the next step.

The next step is John 1:12, "For as many as received Him, to them gave He the right," not power as the old version gives it, but the new word "right," legal right, "to become the sons of God, even to them that believe on His name."

Receiving Jesus Christ is an act of the will, acting on the Word.

You know that you are without a Savior, without approach to God, and without Eternal Life, and you look up to God and say to Him, "God I know I am lost. I know I am spiritually dead and without hope. But I have come to know that Jesus the Nazarene is Your Son, that He died for my sins according to the Scriptures, and that He arose again from the dead because He had legally acquitted me of my guilt and sins. Now I take Him to be my Savior, and I believe You take me to be Your child."

After this prayer, you turn to Romans 10:9, "That if thou shalt confess with thy mouth Jesus as Lord and believe in thy heart that God raised Him from the dead, thou shalt be saved."

Notice this carefully, "'because if thou shalt confess with thy mouth Jesus as Lord."

It is not enough to take Him as your Savior, you must acknowledge His lordship over your life.

The reason for this is very obvious; we have been the servants and subjects as well as children of an enemy of God.

We have belonged to the kingdom or the country of the Devil.

Now we want to leave that country and come into God's country to become naturalized citizens, but before we can do this, we must swear allegiance to our new Fatherland and make an absolute, unconditional break with our old Fatherland.

So he says that we must confess Jesus Christ as Lord, as the new Ruler of our heart-life as well as our intellectual life.

One of the difficulties that will confront us is that we shall wish to have Jesus as Savior but not as our Lord.

Many people want Him as their Savior from Hell, but they don't want Him as their Ruler on earth.

If Jesus becomes your Lord, then He will want to have His say in regard to the class of books you read, the company you keep, the kind of amusements you enjoy, the government of your body, and the kind of a home you make.

He will want to have something to say about your finances, what you do with them, how you make them, and how you use them.

He will want to have something to say in regard to marriage, children, and the home.

He will want to dictate as to your vocation in life and where you live.

Yes, He will want to enter into every department of your life.

This makes the Christian life blessed.

It robs life of its weakness, frailty, and its human guidance, and it lifts it into the realm of the supernatural.

Now that you have received Eternal Life, the nature of the great Father God, seek to govern your life accordingly, and let this new life manifest itself in your daily conduct.

‡ ‡ ‡

Questions

1. Show why the receiving of Eternal Life is the only solution of man's need.
2. Give a definition of the word "Christian."
3. Show why the man in Christ is absolutely a New Creation.
4. For what purpose has the Holy Spirit recorded the Life and death and resurrection of Christ for us?
5. Why is it necessary to acknowledge the Lordship of Christ over our lives when taking Him as Savior?

"The New Birth therefore is not a change of nature as it is sometimes defined; it is rather the communication of the Divine nature. 'Except a man be born from above he cannot see the kingdom of God.' 'Born from above' and very true to fact is this saying. Regeneration is not our natural life carried up to its highest point of attainment, but the Divine life brought down to its lowest point of condescension, even to the heart of fallen man. — It has been the constant dream and delusion of men that they could rise to heaven by development and improvement of their natural life. Jesus by one stroke of revelation destroys this hope, telling His believers that unless he has been begotten of God who is above as truly as he has been begotten of his father on earth, that he cannot see the kingdom of God." — A. J. GORDON.

Chapter The Eleventh

THE NEW BIRTH

HE New Birth is the heart of Christianity.

From the fall of man to Pentecost every plan and purpose in the scheme of Redemption had centered in this.

This is the reason for the Old Testament.

This is the reason for Judaism.

This is the reason for the prophets.

This is the reason for the Incarnation.

This is the reason for the Substitutionary Sacrifice of Jesus.

Here heads up the heart dream of the Eternal Father God.

The integrity of the New Birth is the integrity of the Family.

If we can impugn this fundamental, the whole superstructure from the first sacrifice after the catastrophe in Eden to the Resurrection of Jesus Christ falls in helpless ruin.

It is no wonder that a man's interpretation of the New Birth determines his whole Christian experience.

This is the crux of Christianity.

A denomination is known by its view of the New Birth.

This is no place for human speculation.

The Bible, alone, can settle this question.

If the New Birth is not supernatural, Christianity is one of the religions of the world.

If the New Birth is supernatural, Christianity is a Family and not a religion.

If the New Birth is simply a conversion to new concepts or a theory, then Christianity is purely a human product, blessed or unblessed by God.

This subject is of vital importance so we will investigate it with analytical thoroughness.

THE NEED OF THE NEW BIRTH

It might be well for us to notice first, the need of the New Birth.

Jesus is the first one who speaks of the New Birth, and in His night talk to Nicodemus He tells us with divine accuracy what the New Birth is and the need of it.

Read Jno. 3:1-8.

First, that no one can see or understand the Kingdom of God except he is born from above, that is except the life of God come down into his being.

Second, no one can enter the Kingdom of God except he is born of water and the spirit.

Nicodemus cannot understand it, and then Jesus says, "That which is born of the flesh is flesh, and that which is born of the spirit is spirit; marvel not that I say unto you, ye must be born from above." In the Scripture Jesus shows the difference between the natural and the spiritual man.

One is born of natural generation and the other is born of the Spirit.

Again, Jesus in speaking to the Jews tells them they are of their father, the Devil, that they are partakers of Satanic Nature. (Jno. 8:44-45.)

This with His other statement, that they that believe on Him shall pass out of death into life, shows that Jesus believed man to be spiritually dead, a child of the Devil, and that the New Birth is to be a change of nature which will mean a change of relationship.

Paul tells us in Ephesians 2:1-3, "And you did He make alive, when ye were dead in your trespasses and sins, wherein, ye once walked according to the course of this world, according to the Prince of the powers of the air, of the spirit that now worketh in the sons of disobedience; among whom we also all once lived in the lust of our flesh, doing the desires of the flesh and of the mind, and were by nature children of wrath, even as the rest."

Here man is by Nature a child of wrath; he is spiritually dead, and, in the 12th verse he is "without God," Godless.

He is "without hope," hopeless; he is dead in trespasses; he is separated from Christ.

He belongs to the family of Satan, 1 John 3:10, "In this the children of God are manifest and the children of the Devil."

Because man is a child of the Devil, a partaker of his father's nature, the New Birth is imperative.

He is under condemnation; he has no legal approach to God and cannot approach Him except through the Mediator Jesus Christ.

THE NATURE OF THE NEW BIRTH

Let us look next at the New Testament Teaching of the New Birth, or of a New Birth that is in harmony with the Family Teaching.

First, we will look at the legal side of the New Birth.

LEGAL AND VITAL

Much confusion has been occasioned, because we have not differentiated between the Legal and the Vital sides of the New Birth.

One School of Theology has magnified the Legal side, and another, the Vital.

One has only seen the courthouse aspect, while the other sees but the experimental.

Practically all the great family teachings of Scripture can be understood by the close analogy of our home life.

Marriage is legal and vital.

There is the legal side of the marriage which lays the foundation for the vital, or the experimental union of the two.

THE LEGAL SIDE

The legal part of the New Birth is that portion enacted in the Court House of Heaven.

When the sinner accepts Jesus Christ as his Savior and confesses Him as his Lord, that starts the legal machine in the Court House of Heaven.

First, his sins are Remitted, wiped out as though they had never been.

Second, he is legally Justified or set right with God.

Third, his name is written in the Book of Life, the Family Birthday Book.

Fourth, he is legally Adopted into the Family and this has to be done in the court house.

Fifth, Jesus publicly Confesses him before the Father and the Holy Angels.

Sixth, he is legally Reconciled to the Father.

Seventh, he is declared and made righteous.

A Child's Legal Rights

All legal steps having been taken, now he has first, a legal right to his Father's protection.

Second, he has a legal right to Jesus' intercession.

Third, he has a Legal Right to the Advocacy of Christ, the great Family Lawyer.

Fourth, he has a Legal Right to the gift of the Holy Spirit.

Fifth, he has a Legal Right to a son's place in the Royal Family.

Sixth, he has a Legal Right to a son's inheritance.

Seventh, He has a Legal Right to the use of Jesus' Name.

When you overlook the Legal side of the New Birth, you are rearing an experimental superstructure without a foundation, and the building will surely fall.

This is the reason that so many who teach only the experimental side of the New Birth have so many failures in their congregation—people out of Fellowship.

The Vital Side

This is the work that the Holy Spirit does in the believer when he publicly confesses Christ as Savior and Lord.

First, the Holy Spirit overshadows him.

He is immersed in the Spirit, and this is the real Baptism of the Holy Spirit. (1 Cor. 12:13.)

The receiving of the Holy Spirit into the body comes later.

Second, the Holy Spirit imparts to his spirit the Nature of God, Eternal Life.

This makes him alive in Christ.

Third, the Peace of God that passeth all understanding floods his soul.

Fourth, the Holy Spirit witnesses with his spirit that he is a child of God through the word that says—He has "passed out of death into Life."

Fifth, the Love of God is shed abroad in his heart by the Holy Spirit, and he knows he has passed from Death into Life, because he loves the brethren.

Joy fills his heart, and he cries "Abba, Father," and he knows that he is a child of God, joint-heir with Jesus Christ, the Lord.

There is no leap in the dark here; there is no speculation.

The Legal and the Vital parts of the New Birth are both wrought by God alone.

Man's Part

It will be interesting for us to note now the part Man has to do in this wonderful operation known as the New Birth.

First, he hears the message.

Hearing the message in the Scriptural sense means understanding it.

He comes to know that he is Spiritually dead, a child of the Devil without God and without Hope.

You notice we do not use the word "Believe" or the word "Repent." Believing is really acting on the Word—when you believe or act on the Word you repent, and you do not repent unless you Believe the Word.

Second, he hears of the promise of the Incarnation and the Substitutionary sacrifice of Jesus of Nazareth on his behalf.

Third, he takes Jesus Christ as his Savior and confesses Him before the world as his Lord; and when he does this, God takes him to be His child.

All this is very simple and easily understood.

The moment that this is done God makes him a New Creation, old things pass away, all things have become new, and all things have been wrought of God.

Scriptural Definitions

Jesus says, "He that believeth on me has passed out of death into life."

This is passing out of the realm of Spiritual Death, the Satanic Kingdom, into the realm of Life, the Family of God.

Again Jesus defines it as being "Born from Above."

Birth means Life.

This is divine impartation of the Father's Nature by the energy of the Spirit.

Paul says, "You hath He made alive when you were dead in your trespasses and sins."

This is a statement of fact.

Man is Spiritually Dead! He is a possessor of the nature of the Devil, Spiritual Death, and now he becomes a possessor of the Nature of God, Eternal Life, and the moment that he becomes a possessor of this New Nature he is made Alive; that is, the part of him that was dead is now alive. His spirit was dead—his spirit is now alive.

It does not say one-half alive or partially alive or that he is dead and alive, but that he is made Alive.

John says, "He that hath the Son hath the life; he that hath not the Son of God hath not the life.

"These things have I written unto you, that ye may know that ye have Eternal Life."

This is not a future possession but a present tense possession.

He had Death but now he has Life.

Again John says, "We know that we have passed out of death into life, because we love the brethren.

"He that loveth not abideth in death," and no one that hateth his brother has Eternal Life abiding in him.

Notice three facts.

First, he has passed out of death into life and has a conscious proof of it, in that he loves the brethren.

Second, the man that does not love has not yet passed out of Death, but still abides in the realm of Satan.

Third, no one who hates has Eternal Life abiding in him.

Notice that this Eternal Life is something abiding in the man; it is a present possession.

It has made him Alive.

It is an impartation of God's own Nature or Life to him.

Paul says again, "Wherefore, if any man is in Christ, he is a new creature: the old things are passed away: behold, they are become new, but all things are of God."

Literally, if any man takes Christ as his Savior, that man is a New Creation.

He is not a re-built building, or one who has been fixed over, or one who has received Eternal Life without losing the old nature.

No, Paul says distinctly that he is a New Creation, that the old things, that is the old nature, have passed away, that old structure has been replaced by a new one, and that God has wrought the work Himself.

It is all of God.

THE INTEGRITY OF THE NEW BIRTH

Peter tells us, "Not begotten of corruptible seed but of incorruptible, even the word of God that liveth and abideth forever."

James tells us we are "begotten by the Will of God."

This establishes the integrity of our relationship.

We are not illegitimate children, nor hybrids or half breeds, but we are legitimately born children of God.

Not only are we Legally Born, but we are also legally adopted into God's Family so that our relationship is doubly secure, an actual Birth and a legal Adoption.

THE DUAL THEORY

Many believe that when a man is born again he receives Eternal Life but that the old nature is not removed, and that these natures war with each other in the new creation.

They base this teaching upon the 7th Chapter of Romans.

This is not the experience of a believer but of Paul as a Jew under the Law.

This chapter is a treatise on the Law showing the relation of the Law to the awakened conscience of a Jew, who has not been recreated.

If the reader will turn to this Chapter and read it carefully, he will see that the whole argument is the argument of a Jew before he has been born Again.

He says, "I was alive apart from the law once; but when the commandments came, sin revived, and I died and sin finding occasion, through the commandment beguiled me, and through it slew me."

The believer is not under the Law; he has nothing to do with it whatever.

The Law belongs only to the Jew.

Again he says, "For we know that the Law is spiritual; but I am carnal, sold under sin."

We Gentiles were never under the Jewish Law.

We know that the believer is not sold under sin: he has been made free from sin and has become a bondservant of righteousness.

Again Paul says, "For that which I do I know not: for not what I would, that do I practice; but what I hate, that I do."

This is not the experience of a child of God, "But if what I would not, that I do, I consent unto the law that it is good," (but ye are not under the Law but under grace) so now "it is no more I that do it, but sin which dwelleth in me."

Sin does not dwell in the believer.

Here sin is spoken of as something that was dwelling in Paul.

If sin has a habitation in the believer and the believer is a subject of it, then God is united to sin, or in other words, to the Devil.

"I find then, in regard to the Law, that to me who would do good, evil is present.

"For I delight in the Law of God after the inward man: but I see a different law in my members, warring against the law of my mind, and bringing me into captivity under the law of sin which is in my members."

The Ten Commandments are the Law of Sin; they are the revealer of Sin.

They told the penalty of sin, and Paul delights in this Law from an intellectual point of view but he found another law working in his mind; it was the Law of Sin and Spiritual Death.

Sons Are Freemen

The believer is free from the Dominion of the Law.

The believer is free from the Dominion of Sin.

The believer is free from the Dominion of Spiritual Death.

The believer is free from the Dominion of Satan.

The believer is now under the Dominion of the Grace of God, and Jesus is his Lord.

Could a child of God utter this cry? "Wretched man that I am! who shall deliver me out of the body of this death?"

That is not the language of a child of God; that is the language of a Jew under the Law who has seen his actual condition and has also seen the possibilities of Redemption in Christ Jesus our Lord.

In Gal. 5:16-18 is another proof-text of the Dual Nature Theorist, "But I say, Walk by the Spirit, and ye shall not fulfill the lust of the flesh.

"For the flesh lusteth against the Spirit, and the Spirit against the flesh; for these are contrary the one to the other, that ye may not do the things that ye would.

"But if ye are led by the Spirit, ye are not under the law."

Contrast

In this Epistle Paul is contrasting the Jew under the Law and the believer under Grace, for the Book of Galatians is a book of contrasts.

It is a contrast of Law and and Grace.

It is a contrast of Faith and Works.

It is a contrast of Sons and Servants.

It is a contrast of Circumcision and the New Birth.

It is a contrast of Promise and Law, of Flesh and Spirit, that is Natural Man and Spiritual Man.

It is a contrast of Christianity and Judaism.

It is a contrast of Love and Legality.

We know that Man is a spirit.

We know that he lives in a physical body.

We know that nearly all the sins that are committed are committed through physical senses.

We know that these physical senses can become distorted, dissipated, abnormal so that they will crave unnatural gratification.

We know that the believer's life is a battle with his physical body.

The reason for this is that we are not normal human beings.

Parental sins have set our teeth on edge.

We are living in the realm of Spiritual Death where Satan is the Emperor.

Evil suggestions and temptations are in the very air we breathe.

Most of the people with whom we associate are under the Dominion of the Devil.

Satan's appeal always comes through the physical senses; so Man's only hope is to live in the spirit.

I don't mean the Holy Spirit, but in his own spirit realm; instead of dreaming of gratifying physical passions or desires, he is to live in the realm of the spiritual, his own spirit fellowshipping with the Spirit of God.

This is the only way to overcome the influence of his physical body upon himself. So Paul says here, "If we walk by the spirit," more literally, if we walk in the realm of the spirit, "ye shall not fulfill the lust of the flesh," for the members of your body are combating against your spirit, and your spirit is contending against your flesh or the members of your body.

TEMPTATION AND SIN

The cries of your perverted physical body are not sin, but if you yield to them it is sin. Every appeal of Satan will come on this level; so there is going to be a combat until your physical body is brought into subjection to your spirit. But if you let the Holy Spirit dominate your spirit He will lead you out into liberty and victory over these temptations. He will bring your physical body into perfect submission; so that your life will be tranquil, pure, and victorious.

Paul says in Romans: "Let not sin therefore reign in your mortal body, that ye should obey the lusts thereof: neither present your members unto sin as instruments of unrighteousness; but present yourselves unto God, as alive from the dead, and your members as instruments of righteousness unto God."

He is bringing the same truth to the Roman believers.

They have been Born Again, are New Creations, free from the Dominion of Sin, Satan, and the Law. He says, "I don't want you to let sin reign as King in this death-doomed body of yours; neither do I want you to present your members unto sin as weapons of unrighteousness against your spirit but present yourselves unto God as alive from the dead and your members as weapons of righteousness."

You are living in the physical body.

Your spirit and soul are operating through the members of your body, namely: your eyes, your ears, your mouth, your hands, your feet, your organs, and your appetite.

Practically all the sins in the world today are sins connected with these members.

The whole combat of your life today is to bring these members under perfect control so that they do not break the fellowship between your spirit and the Holy Spirit.

He who knows how to control his tongue, his passions, and appetites will live a blameless life in this crooked and perverse generation.

Dual Nature Dilemma

There is nothing wrong in the physical body, but if you turn it over to the Devil and allow him to work through it, it will destroy the spirit.

God gave us our body as a servant; we are to rule it, but if the servant rules us, it is anarchy and confusion.

If man is not a New Creation but simply receives a New Nature plus the old Nature, we are led into a strange dilemma.

We know that this old Nature is Satanic Nature, Spiritual Death; then the man who has received this New Nature has two Natures, the Nature of God and the Nature of the Devil.

He belongs to two families, the Family of God and the family of the Devil.

Satan has a legal right to rule over his part of the Nature, and God has a legal right to rule over His part.

This gives to man a double nature; One is Doctor Jekyll, and the other is Mr. Hyde: legally a child of God, and legally a child of the Devil.

To follow this out logically, one half of man can go to Hell, and the other half, to Heaven.

The Theory would be humorous if it were not so serious; but the problem is when does man get rid of this Satanic nature.

Their answer is, at Death.

We know that Death is of the Devil; this leads us into a still worse dilemma.

If this is so, the sacrifice of Jesus Christ has failed in its object.

The man who has accepted Him as his Savior is only partly saved, and he is not redeemed.

Satan still has a legal right to rule over him.

Jesus Christ is obliged to divide His Dominion with the Devil.

This is humiliating.

The Fall of Man was a finished product; the Redemption is a fumble.

The New Birth is a hybrid, a bitter failure.

The humiliating part of it is that according to this theory God is obliged to seek the Devil's assistance in order to perfect Man.

Death, the first child of Satan, is to put the finishing touches on the New Creation, God's child. If Man is cleansed or made free from the Adamic Nature by Physical Death, why was it that God did not permit Physical Death to save the whole human race, for all die?

This thing is too abhorrent to even contemplate.

It makes God justify a child of the Devil or a hybrid at the best.

It makes God unite Himself with the Devil in the human.

It makes Jesus' statement, "I am the vine, ye are the branches" grotesque.

It makes Satan, our destroyer, in the end our redeemer.
The heart shrinks from this teaching.

We believe that the New Birth is a New Birth.

We believe that the New Creation is a New Creation.

We believe that God was able to do as finished a work in Man's Redemption as the Devil did in his Destruction.

We believe that the New Birth glorifies God, magnifies Jesus Christ, and exalts the human.

It is not a desirable task to array one's self against the common teachings of the Church, especially of those who are among the most devout and deeply zealous of all the Family of God, and I know that my readers recognize that I do not come to these great experimental teachings of the Church with the spirit of resentment or hostility, but as a fellow-member of the body of Christ who believes he has an answer to these problems that have agitated the Church during the last hundred years.

The writer loves the members of the Family as he loves himself and would speak with the freedom that love gives on these great themes.

The fact that in the new birth we actually receive the nature of God has not been majored by the Church. This has led us into many difficulties as we have already seen.

One very devout group talks much about Justification and Adoption.

It would seem as though the fact of the New Creation, as a New Creation, had never been given serious consideration.

They teach that when one accepts Jesus Christ as Savior that God justifies him of all that he ever did; that is, He forgives him of his sins, but He does not remove the sin nature, the cause of his sins.

This step which is called conversion, is considered simply a preliminary.

The real work is known as the Second Work of Grace, or being Wholly Sanctified.

This Second Work comes to the convert only when he has surrendered himself utterly to the Lord, has repented deeply, and has sought diligently for a clean heart.

They do not believe that the heart is made clean at conversion, as that term is used.

They make a distinction between sin and sins.

Sin, is what we are by nature; sins, what we do.

Many of their teachers have believed that when one is converted he receives the Holy Spirit in a limited measure, and when he becomes wholly Sanctified the Spirit fills the temple.

They also teach that one can lose this gracious blessing of a clean heart, or Sanctification, by the slightest known sin.

For this reason the majority of those who go to the altar and honestly seek for this blessing lose it in a few weeks or months after the struggle for it.

Those who are familiar with Mr. Wesley's Journal remember that he was confronted with this same difficulty when he returned in his itinerancy, that in some places many who had received this Second Work of Grace and rejoiced greatly in its reception, were found under a cloud, backslidden, and the work needed to be done again.

This teaching has produced an unstable and vacillating type of Christianity.

It has made the recipient skeptical of himself and others.

It has not been a healthful teaching, but it has produced in the face of all this, by the Grace of God, some very devout Christians.

‡   ‡   ‡

Questions

1. Show why every purpose in Redemption from the fall of man to the day of Pentecost centers in the New Birth.

2. Explain the legal side of the New Birth.

3. Explain the vital side of the New Birth.

4. Why is it impossible for a man to be Born Again and yet retain the old nature?

5. Through what is our combat with sin after we have been Born Again?

"The Comforter in every part of his three-fold work glorifies Christ. In convincing of sin he convinces us of the sin of not believing on Christ. In convincing us of righteousness he convinces us of the righteousness of Christ, of that righteousness which was made manifest in Christ's going to the Father and which he received to bestow on all such as should believe in Him. And lastly, in convincing of judgment, he convinced us that the Prince of the World was judged in the life and by the death of Christ. Thus, throughout, Christ is glorified; and that which the Comforter shows to us relates in all its parts to the life and work of the Incarnate Son of God." — JULIUS CHARLES HART.

Chapter The Twelfth

THE HOLY SPIRIT

HIS has been called the Age or Dispensation of the Holy Spirit.

When Jesus was about to leave the disciples, He promised that He would send the Holy Spirit into the world to become their Teacher, Guide, and Comforter.

This coming Being was going to have charge of the ministry and the work of the Church.

He was going to guide the Church as a whole, and guide its members as individuals.

He was to overshadow the Church, and they were to walk in His presence.

He was to come also into the individual member's body to take up His abode there so that He might govern his actions, think through his mind, love through his affections, and will through his will. His body was to be His permanent home.

Under the old dispensation, He had dwelt between the Cherubim in the Holy of Holies; now He is to dwell in the soul and spirit of man, this new tabernacle of flesh.

First, I want you to notice that the Holy Spirit is a person.

In Matt. 28:19 Jesus says, "Go ye into all the world and make disciples of all the nations, baptizing them in the name of the Father, and of the Son, and of the Holy Spirit."

Here Jesus gives the Holy Spirit the same place, the same personality, and the same honor that He gives to the Father and to Himself.

In 1 Cor. 2:10-14, "But unto us God revealed them through the Spirit; for the Spirit searcheth all things, yea, the deep things of God.

"For who among men knoweth the things of a man, save the spirit of the man, which is in him? even so the things of God none knoweth, save the Spirit of God."

163

"Which things also we speak, not in words which man's wisdom teacheth, but which the Spirit teacheth; combining spiritual things with spiritual words.

"Now the natural man receiveth not the things of the Spirit of God: for they are foolishness unto him; and he cannot know them, because they are spiritually understood."

Here, the Spirit is the searcher of the deep things of God.

He is the teacher of the Church, and He knows the mind of God, and He reveals that mind of God to the individual child of God.

This perfectly agrees with what Jesus said in John 16: That the Holy Spirit was to convict the world of Sin, of Righteousness, and of Judgment, and that He was to guide us into all truth for He should not speak from Himself but of whatsoever things He heard. "These shall He speak; and He shall declare unto you the things that are to come. He shall glorify me; for He shall take of mine, and shall declare it unto you."

In these ministries the Spirit reveals an intellect that thinks and guides.

In Romans 15:30 Paul speaks of the "love of the Spirit," and in Romans 5:5 he says that "the love of God is shed abroad in our hearts by the Holy Spirit."

By these Scriptures we infer that the Holy Spirit is the channel through which this new wonderful love nature of God is revealed to the individual members of the Body of Christ.

Again in 1 Cor. 12:11 Paul says that these various gifts are distributed "severally, even as He wills."

In other words, the Holy Spirit has the guidance and the plans for the Church, and He gives to one man the gift of wisdom, to another the gift of knowledge, to one the gift of healing, and to another the gift of tongues; but He divides these as He pleases, for His will is sovereign.

Jesus has honored the Holy Spirit by giving Him a position of equality with the Father, not as a Spirit that emanates from the Father, but an individual personality who has intellect, sensibilities, and will.

We believe the Holy Spirit to be a person.

The Holy Spirit is not an emanation from the Spirit of God.

God is a person with intellect, sensibilities, and will.

By way of illustration, we speak of the spirit of a man; that spirit cannot leave a man; it is a part of his personality.

The Scriptures speak of the Spirit of Christ: "If a man has not the Spirit of Christ, he is none of His."

The Spirit of Christ mentioned here is not the Holy Spirit, but it is Christ's own Spirit, a part of His own individual personality.

The Holy Spirit is a distinct being, a personality distinct from God the Father, and God the Son.

Operating in His own sphere, having His own personality, the Holy Spirit is different from the Father and the Son in this respect. The Son now has a human body and is seated at the right hand of the Father, and the Father holds His place on the Eternal Throne.

The Spirit's special place of activity today is on earth, convicting of sin, holding back the powers of darkness, recreating members of the Family of God, and guiding, comforting, and indwelling their bodies.

The Holy Spirit's home is the Human body.

"Know ye not that your body is the temple of the Holy Spirit."

"Greater is He that is in you than he that is in the world."

In the Old Testament times the Holy Spirit's work as indicated in the Scriptures was in creation, renewing the face of the earth, inspiring men to write the Holy Oracles of God, and coming upon men for special operations and special works of might and leadership.

His permanent home then was in the tabernacle, afterward, the Temple.

The Holy Spirit did not make His permanent abode in the body of man then, because man was spiritually dead, a child of the Devil, though he lived under the Blood Covenant and was sheltered by the Atonement Blood.

He could not make His home in the human body until man had been recreated. This could not take place until Christ had come and paid the penalty of sin, taken His seat as Mediator, and sent Eternal Life to the men who would take Him as Savior.

The Holy Spirit's work today is: first, that of a convicter of the world.

He does this through the preached Word, through the Living Word in the lives of believers, through the written word, the Scriptures, or religious literature.

His work in the individual members of the Family of God is that of a Teacher, Guide, Comforter, Overcomer, and Sanctifier.

The Holy Spirit's real home is in the heart of God's Children, but He does not come into every believer at the New Birth.

The New Birth is receiving the life, the nature of God.

This makes him a child of God and a human temple of the Holy Spirit to indwell.

After he is born again, he has a legal right to ask the Holy Spirit to come into his body to take possession of it.

RECEIVING THE HOLY SPIRIT

This subject has recently been a bone of contention in the Theological world.

There is as much confusion about this as about the New Birth, but a clear understanding of the Word in regard to the New Birth makes this subject easy to understand.

The New Birth is receiving Eternal Life, Justification, and Adoption.

Receiving the Holy Spirit is simply inviting the person of the Holy Spirit to come into these bodies of ours after we have been Born Again to make them His permanent abode.

The sinner does not want the Holy Spirit; he wants a Savior and Eternal Life. So Jesus says in John 14:16-17, "And I will pray the Father, and he shall give you another Comforter, that he may be with you forever, even the Spirit of truth: whom the world cannot receive; for it beholds him not, neither knoweth him; ye know him; for he abideth with you, and shall be in you."

Notice first, that the world cannot receive Him.

Here the world means unregenerated man.

Second, that He was abiding with the disciples who had not been Born Again.

They were simply Jews under the Law until Christ had paid the penalty of their sin and sent Eternal Life to them by the Holy Spirit on the Day of Pentecost.

Third, Jesus says, "He shall be in you."

Notice the tense is future.

In Luke 11:13 Jesus says, "If ye then being evil, know how to give good gifts unto your children, how much more shall your heavenly Father give the Holy Spirit to them that ask Him?"

You will notice here, first, that it is the Father giving the Holy Spirit to His children.

Second, the Holy Spirit is given to the children who ask.

Third, the inference is that only children of God are eligible to receive the Holy Spirit.

The Testimony of Acts

The Book of Acts is the final authority on this subject.

What did the Apostles do and teach?

In Peter's sermon on the Day of Pentecost he concluded with this, "Repent ye, and be baptized every one of you in the name of Jesus Christ unto remission of your sins, and ye shall receive the gift of the Holy Spirit."

Notice here that he says they are to receive Remission of Sins and the Gift of the Holy Spirit.

See how perfectly this harmonizes with their practice in the coming days.

After the dispersion that was caused by the death of Stephen, Philip goes down to Samaria and begins to preach.

The city turned to the Lord, and the people were baptized, both men and women.

"Now when the apostles that were at Jerusalem heard that Samaria had received the word of God, they sent unto them Peter and John: who when they were come down prayed for them, that they might receive the Holy Spirit: for as yet it was fallen upon none of them: only they had been baptized into the name of the Lord Jesus.

"Then laid they their hands on them, and they received the Holy Spirit."

Notice how it reads, "Then laid they their hands on them, and they received the Holy Spirit."

This is apostolic practice.

First, men were born into the Family, baptized, and then hands were laid upon them, and they definitely received the Holy Spirit into their bodies.

Again in Acts 19:1-7, "And it came to pass that while Apollos was at Corinth, Paul having passed through the upper country came to Ephesus, and found certain disciples: and he said unto them, Did ye receive the Holy Spirit when ye believed? And they said unto him, Nay, we did not so much as hear whether the Holy Spirit was given. And he said, Into what, then were ye baptized. And they said, Into John's baptism. And Paul said, John baptized with the baptism of repentance saying unto the people that they should believe on him that should come after him, that is on Jesus. And when they had heard this, they were baptized into the name of the Lord Jesus. And when Paul had laid his hands upon them, the Holy Spirit came on them: and they spake with tongues, and prophesied." (These were converts of John the Baptist—Knew nothing of redemption in Jesus.)

Notice how Paul says, "Did ye receive the Holy Spirit when ye believed," indicating that there were some who believed but did not receive the Holy Spirit, and after he had preached Christ to them they were baptized, and he laid his hands upon them and they received the Holy Spirit.

This is all very simple and normal, easily understood, easily done.

They are children of God and as children they have a legal right to the indwelling presence of the Holy Spirit in their bodies.

The Reason

The reason that the Holy Spirit comes into our bodies is: first, that God can empower us to resist the temptations of the Devil best by living in our bodies.

This Scripture then becomes true: "Greater is He that is in you than he that is in the world."

Second, that He may be our Teacher, Guide, and Comforter.

Third, that He may empower us for testimony and service.

Fourth, that He may make the Father and Jesus real to our spirits.

One reason for the weakness of the Church today is that the Holy Spirit is simply with them and not in them.

It is not Sanctification that we want or a clean heart, or a blessing, or a new experience, but it is the Person, Holy Spirit.

How He Comes In

First, we know that we are God's children.

Second, we are living in fellowship with Him.

Third, we recognize the Lordship of Jesus over our lives.

Fourth, we know that we have a legal right to His indwelling.

Fifth, in simple confidence we go to the Father and ask Him in Jesus' name to give us the Holy Spirit, and He will as truly as He gave us Eternal Life when we took Christ as our Savior, for His Word cannot be broken.

"How much more shall your heavenly Father give the Holy Spirit to them that ask Him."

Questions

1. In this dispensation what is the home of the Holy Spirit?

2. What is the ministry of the Holy Spirit today?

3. Why is it that the Holy Spirit could not make His abode in the body of man under the Old Covenant?

4. How does one receive the Holy Spirit?

5. What will the Holy Spirit do for us when he comes in?

"A new commandment I give unto you, that ye love one another; even as I have loved you, that ye also love one another. By this shall all men know that ye are my disciples, if ye love one another." Jn. 13:34-35.

"Beloved, let us love one another: for love is of God; and every one that loveth is begotten of God, and knoweth God. He that loveth not knoweth not God; for God is love. Herein was the love of God manifested in us, that God hath sent his only begotten Son into the world that we might live through him. Herein is love, not that we loved God, but that he loved us, and sent his Son to be the propitiation for our sins. Beloved, if God so loved us, we also ought to love one another." 1 Jn. 4:7-11.

"And we know and have believed the love which God hath in us. God is love; and he that abideth in love abideth in God, and God abideth in him." 1 Jn. 4:16.

Chapter The Thirteenth

THE NEW LAW OF THE FAMILY

ESUS was always revolutionary; He was never commonplace.

Regardless of the angle from which you study the life of Jesus, you find that He is not ordinary.

He never accommodated Himself to the errors, the fashions, nor the theories of the age in which He lived.

He came as a witness of the Truth.

He Himself was the Truth!

The word we have translated "truth," in its heart meaning, is reality.

That word expresses Jesus better than any other English word.

Jesus was Reality!

He was the embodiment of divine reality, and every subject on which He expressed Himself is a revelation.

His whole ministry and life ran counter to the age in which He lived, as well as to this age.

Jesus would be as much a stranger today as He was when He first appeared upon the horizon of Israel.

His new law which is to govern the family is expressed in John 13:34-35, "A new commandment I give unto you, that ye love one another; even as I have loved you, that ye also love one another. By this shall all men know that ye are my disciples, if ye have love one for another."

Jesus sometimes was startling, unique in His expression.

Here it would seem that He coined a word.

He wanted to express something, and there was no Greek word in current use available.

He had brought to the world a new thing, something that had been lost since the Fall.

It was the old Edenic Love that had been displaced by hatred.

There had been a verb used, but no noun.

The verb is agapao, but Jesus gives them the noun agapa. (We are anglicizing the Greek word Agape.)

This was a new kind of Love.

You see it was a new Family, with a new Nature, with a new Father.

They were New people; they must have language that would fit this new kingdom, this new Family.

They had been translated out of the Kingdom of Darkness into the Kingdom of the Son of His Love, and in this new realm they must have a language befitting.

They must have laws befitting, and so He says, "A new commandment give I unto you."

What is it?

That ye have "agapa" one for another even as I have had "agapa" for you.

I can see the disciples looking at one another, and John says to Peter, "Say, this is a new kind of love."

Peter shakes his head and says, "Yes, but I don't understand it. It is a puzzle to me. He is bringing so many new things that it confuses me. One moment He is talking about Eternal Life, then about the Father, and now of this new word agapa. What does He mean?"

Peter never understood it until Pentecost.

We catch a glimpse of it in Rom. 5:5, "The love of God is shed abroad in our hearts by the Holy Spirit."

What is this that is shed abroad?

It is the love of God.

It is the Nature of God, manifesting itself.

Vegetable Life in the peach tree manifests itself first, in the leaf, then the blossom, then the luscious fruit.

The Nature of God, Eternal Life, will manifest itself likewise in the Nature, Conduct, and Speech of the child of God.

When one is born from above, the Father's Nature comes into his spirit.

That Nature is bound to manifest itself in Love.

It will be Divine Love which is so radically different from our Old Human Love that we can hardly call it Love, although it operates through the same faculties.

When the Church was born on Pentecost, the phenomena of the Jews' deliberately giving their property away and performing other acts as strange were the first manifestation of this new kind of Love that had come to earth.

I think it would be well for us at this point to contrast it with another Greek word.

AGAPA AND PHILEO

The Common Greek word in use in Jesus' day was Phileo, which means human love. It is the love of a mother for her child, the love of a husband for his wife.

This was the highest type of love that man had ever felt.

There were Greek terms that differentiated between natural love and lusts, but there was no other word for a higher kind of love than Phileo.

This common human love of ours is the most blessed asset of the human, and yet, the most dangerous.

This Phileo love is the Goddess of the divorce court. It is the High Priestess of human suffering. It is the parent of most of our tears, sorrows, and heart agonies.

It turns to jealousy and murder at the slightest pretext.

It has caused more headlines in the daily papers than all other human passions.

It is the underlying cause of human failure.

It is purely selfish. It feeds only upon self-gratification.

Jesus brings a new kind of love, a love that seeketh not its own.

This in itself is so revolutionary that we in this generation can scarcely credit it.

This new kind of love is the real interpretation of the heart nature of God.

Human love is the interpretation of the human; this new kind of love is the interpretation of God.

This old love springs from the natural heart. This new love springs from the recreated heart.

One is the manifestation of natural man, and the other, the manifestation of God in the new man.

Agapa is tender, forbearing, full of long suffering and kindness. It is absolutely unselfish, seeking only the joy and welfare of others.

Human love can't do this. You may talk glibly about it, but after all self is the center around which it must ever move.
Agapa has a new center.

This center is outside of itself. It is God.

Phileo has utterly failed.

We have the statement of Scriptures that Agapa never fails. Agapa is God's acting through the lives of His children.

There can be no Agapa manifestation today except through those who have become partakers of the Divine nature.

There is no such thing as a synthetic Agapa. It is one thing that cannot be duplicated. It is the genius and badge of Christianity. It is God's manifestation in the flesh. It is the heart of God throbbing in the human.

All other religions break down here; the best they have is Phileo, clothed perchance in new garments but the same old broken human love.

Agapa is not only the law of the family, but it is also the life of the family and the joy of the family.

It makes Christianity more beautiful than any of the so-called religions of the earth.

It makes the life of the Saints the sweetest and most fragrant of all the human.

Its prayer under persecution is "Father, forgive them for they know not what they do."

It breathes the fragrance of forgiveness.

It is bravery clothed in humility.

It is strength clothed in gentleness.

It is the bond which binds the family together and makes the strong bear the burdens of the weak, the rich pay the bills of the poor, the cultured become the companion of the ignorant.

It is Christ again manifest among men.

It compels a new vocabulary to express itself.

It has no need of the adjectives of satire, of hatred, or of jealousy.

No thorns grow on its roses, and no poison lurks in its blossoms.

It is the heart of God pulsating 'on the lips of His children.

It makes home, heaven.

The Contrast

As Leviticus was an Exposition of the law of the First Covenant — so 1 Cor. 13 is an Exposition of the New Law.

Paul sums up the difference between Phileo and Agapa in his great poem, the 13th Chapter of 1 Corinthians.

"If I speak with the tongues of men and of angels but have not agapa, I am become sounding brass, or a clanging cymbal."

Paul was a great scholar and knew that the linguistic gift was one of the most highly prized.

He says, "If I understand all the languages of the earth, and if I am able to decipher the hieroglyphics on monuments reared by the forgotten nations, if I am able to understand the language of the angelic hosts, but have not Agapa, I am become sounding brass or a clanging cymbal."

This strips Christianity of its verbal garment and leaves it standing naked.

This gives the reason for the empty churches, the failure of the Sunday School to hold its army of young people, and the failure of Christianity in business and social life.

Men have become mere sounding brass and clanging cymbals.

This tells why the modern religious periodical goes begging for subscribers.

Sounding brass, clanging cymbal, empty words, words, words, words; ever words, only words, empty words.

The heart searches through them for meat, but it only finds the husks, the chaff.

How the hungry heart of the human is crying to the Church for Agapa; nothing else it has can satisfy.

"And if I have the gift of prophecy and know all mysteries and all knowledge but have not Agapa, I am nothing."

Paul is revealing another universal desire of man, the gift of prophecy, the ability to foretell the future events, to know the solution of the great world problems, of the divisions of the nations, the outcome of the strife between capital and labor, and the solution of the social problem.

If one had the gift to read the future, no building ever erected would hold the people who would throng to hear him speak.

No author has ever been paid per word the immense sum that this writer could demand and get.

He may possess this wonderful gift; yet if he does not have agapa, God says, and his words drip with tenderness and tears, "he is nothing."

"And if one knows all mysteries and has all knowledge," Oh, Paul, you are getting down into the heart of us now — how we have craved knowledge; how we have yearned to roll up the curtain and look behind the scenes and there read the revelation of the mysteries that surround us; how we have longed to know how to obtain electricity without friction, to tap the hidden streams of that mighty fluid that flows through the universe, to solve the problem of revitalization of the soil; yes, yes, and the thousands of unknown but imperatively needed utilities to bless the world.

Paul tells us that though we know all these things but do not have Agapa, "we are nothing."

How this awakens, how this startles, how this hurts!

Again Paul says, "If I have all faith so as to remove mountains, but have not Agapa I am nothing."

How we have worshipped at the altar of the linguist, the God of prophecy and knowledge, how we have struggled for this mountain-moving faith and yet this man, Paul, strikes one blow that shatters all our day dreams and cuts the taproot of our ambition.

Knowledge, wisdom, faith, languages, all these are the things that the scholastic world is seeking today.

Paul tells us we may have them all, the universities of the world may rise up and acclaim us the uncrowned kings of the scholastic world; yet he whispers in our ear, "you are nothing unless Agapa rules your life."

This is God's epitaph upon the dead churches of today.

Scholarship has never been able to take the place of Agapa.

"And if I bestow all my goods to feed the poor and give my body to be burned," that is, if one were able to feed the poor of this generation, to rear libraries and hospitals in every city and town and if one wears his body out in philanthropic endeavor and yet does not have Agapa, it profits him nothing; he has wasted his life, it is poured out like water upon a sand-pile.

What is the thing without which human endeavors, human learning, human achievements, are failures?

Oh! it is this new love, the revelation of the heart of God that Jesus brought to the earth.

It is a revelation, but it is more. It is the life of God outpoured in our hearts, manifesting itself through our words and conduct.

It is the pulsation of the heart of God, manifesting itself in an atmosphere that comes from our spirits, blessing and comforting a needy world.

It is God's answer to the despairing cry of the broken-hearted human.

Paul tells us that "Agapa suffereth long and is kind."

Phileo may suffer, but it grows bitter under the burden.

"Agapa envieth not."

Phileo has always manifested itself in envy and jealousy.

"Agapa vaunteth not itself, is not puffed up."

Phileo has forever vaunted itself. Self is the center around which it moves.

If you take selfishness from Phileo, it would crumble and fall to the ground; that is its very strength.

"Agapa does not behave itself unseemly."

Phileo airs its grievances in the divorce court. It grows wildly jealous and strikes down in cold blood the object of its affection.

Phileo is loud-mouthed and often vulgar.

"Agapa seeketh not its own."

The struggle of Phileo from its birth to its death is to get and hold its own.

It is unhappy. It is miserly. It becomes dishonest and treacherous. Its motto is "all things are fair in love and war."

It is a cruel despot, but it is the best this old human had from the fall until Jesus came.

"Agapa is not provoked."

Phileo is sensitive and difficult to handle. It is easily provoked. It tells us that it is very sensitive and must not be neglected or rudely shocked.

Sensitiveness is and always has been of the Devil.

"Agapa taketh not account of evil."

Phileo is always discussing and feasting upon the scandals of the world.

"Agapa rejoiceth not in unrighteousness but rejoiceth with the truth."

Phileo cannot understand this. It turns to hatred and revenge at the slightest provocation, and it always rejoices in the fall of its enemy, and it cannot rejoice with the truth if that truth does not gratify its passion.

"Agapa beareth all things, believeth all things, hopeth all things, endureth all things."

Agapa never goes bankrupt.

Phileo squanders its fortune in its youth in riotous living, and before it comes to manhood's strength, it is in danger of being dashed upon the rocks of failure.

What is Agapa?

John tells us that God is Agapa.

In other words this new thing that Jesus brought to the world is the nature of the great Creator God, which He intended should permeate all creation. He intended that it should rule animals and that it should be the nature of the human, but with the Fall, Spiritual Death took its place, and out of this awful nature of the Devil springs Hatred, Revenge, and Unbelief.

A spirit of restlessness grips all nature.

Man and beast, today, are dominated by this foreign, unnatural power; and yet the heart of the animal and the heart of the human are sobbing for Agapa; when the strong will no longer feed upon the weak — the poor will no longer be exploited by the rich, and God shall rule over all.

Agapa, is the New Law of the Church, the Family of God.

Reader, does Agapa govern you, or are you still dominated by the old corrupt human love?

‡   ‡   ‡

Questions

1. Why was it necessary for a new law to be given to the New Creation?

2. Why is the nature of God bound to manifest itself in love in our conduct?

3. Define "Phileo."

4. Define "Agapa."

5. Discuss the comparison of "Phileo" and "Agapa" as given in 1 Corinthians, the thirteenth chapter.

"Christ, if we may say it reverently, became mystically a babe again on the day of Pentecost, and the hundred and twenty were His infantile body, as once more through the Holy Spirit He incarnated Himself in flesh. Now He is growing and increasing in His members and so will He continue to do 'till we all come in the unity of the faith and of the knowledge of the Son of God unto a perfect man, unto the measure of the stature of the fullness of Christ' — The glorified Christ manifests Himself to man through His Body. If there is a perfect correspondence between Himself and His members, then there will be a true manifestation of Himself. Therefore does the Spirit abide in the body, that the body may be 'in-Christed', that is indwelt by Christ and transfigured into the likeness of Christ. Only thus as 'a chosen generation, a royal priesthood, a holy nation, a peculiar people' can it show forth the virtues of Him who has called us out of darkness into His marvelous light."
— A. J. GORDON.

Chapter The Fourteenth

THE HOUSEHOLD OF GOD

HE family fact is the basic fact of all Scripture. The primal dream of the Creator God was a Family of sons and daughters, on whose love and response, His spirit, His heart nature, could feed.

Rotherham translates Ephesians 1:5, "In love marking us out beforehand unto sonship through Jesus Christ unto Himself."

God marked us out for the position and place of sons in His Family.

This Family fact brings clearly to the front this great truth, that man is an eternal being.

He could not have been a son of God and a partaker of His nature unless he was like God, and being like God he would be eternal and in God's class.

Perhaps the most wonderful fact is that God did not create the whole human race by one word of His power, but He created one man and one woman and permitted them to be the father and mother of His children.

He takes humanity into partnership with Himself, and lets us give birth to His joy.

This shows the eternal responsibility of fatherhood and motherhood.

He could have created the whole human race at one time, but this He did not choose to do.

He preferred to let us have the pleasure of fellowshipping with Him in it.

In Galatians 6:10, Paul lays down a law in regard to the Family: "So then as we have opportunity let us work that which is good toward all men and especially toward them that are of the Household of Faith."

The Faith Family

Here God's Family is given a very choice name, "the Household of Faith," the Family of Faith.

They are beautiful titles, revealing that we are blood-brothers; we have partaken of the same nature, and we are heirs and joint-heirs of Jesus Christ.

We are God's Family representatives on the earth.

We are not Methodists, Baptists, Episcopalians, or Roman Catholics, but we are God's sons and daughters, God's Family.

As members of the Family, we are to minister to each other and watch over each other in love.

In Ephesians 2:19, "So then ye are no more strangers and sojourners, but ye are fellow citizens with the Saints of the Household of God."

We are God's Household! He is to live with us!

Jesus said, "If a man love me, he will keep my word, My Father will love him, and we will come unto him and make our home with him." Jn. 14:23.

God desires to live with His children.

He does not want to be simply a guest in our home.

He wants to have a Father's place in our lives and hearts.

It is a very precious promise that Jesus makes, that He and the Father will come and make their home with us.

They could then become the Burden-bearers, the Comforters, and we could depend upon their wisdom and protection in all of life's hard struggles.

The Father's attitude toward us is given by Jesus, when He says, "The Father Himself loveth you." Jn. 16:27.

The Father God Himself yearns over us tenderly, loves us.

In Revelation 3:20 Jesus shows us how He longs to come into our homes and sit at the table with us, to feast with us. (Eating together in that great eastern country is a very sacred privilege), and He says, "Behold, I stand at the door and knock; if any man hear my voice and will open the door, I will come in to him, and will sup with him, and he with me," fellowshipping on mutual ground.

How it would change our homes, if He did literally dwell in them!

How much bitterness and unkindness that mar them today would then be absent!

If Christians could only realize that it is a Family affair instead of denominational, the Father would mean more to them, and they would be able to bring greater joy to Him.

Ephesians 3:14-15, "For this cause I bow my knees unto the Father, from whom every Family in Heaven and on earth is named."

All fatherhoods head up in the great Father God in Heaven, and notice it said, "Every family on earth and in Heaven," ours is a Heavenly Family.

The Greek used here for Family is "Fatherhood," the fatherhood instinct of animal creation was given it by God . . . All fatherhood love in the human comes out of the great bosom of our Father God.

He is the fountain of Fatherhoods.

Yet in the face of all these facts, should you go to one of our ordinary Prayer Meetings throughout all our vast number of Churches, you would hardly hear the name of Father mentioned once; it is just God; He is only God today.

The Churches are simply orphan asylums of fatherless children who are seeking blindly to get into Heaven, and while they stay on earth they try to get Him to bless and help when they are in trial or need, but He is not a Father.

He has no Father place in their hearts, and they are not children in heart.

They have imbibed the servant spirit, and they talk about being servants of God, but never about being sons.

And whenever they speak of the New Birth, they speak of it as adoption not as birth.

They even carry it from their teachings, into their lives; they are only adopted children.

They have not partaken of the divine nature; they have not escaped the corruption of the world which comes through union with the Devil.

If they are sons, they are like the oldest son in the story of the Prodigal, who lived with the servants with only a servant spirit.

No sadder feature of the modern Church can be imagined: the children of God Almighty have taken the place of servants, utterly ignorant of their sonship privileges or responsibilities.

Paul writes in 1 Timothy 3:15, "that thou mayest know how men ought to behave themselves in the House of God, which is the church of the Living God, the pillar and ground, (or stay) of the truth."

"How we ought to behave ourselves," not in a Church building when we come together for services or fellowship, but in the Family, ·the Household of God; that may mean in your work, or in your pleasures; it may mean in the Assembly of the Family.

Paul is writing to tell us how we ought to act toward the Brethren, toward the Sisters, toward the young and aged, in this wonderful Household of Faith, this Family of God.

How few know how to behave themselves!

How few understand the etiquette of the Royal Family!

How few appreciate their privileges or responsibilities toward each other!

This Family is the pillar, the ground, or more literally, the depository of all truth that is in the world today.

Paul makes us to understand something that some of us have come to know: that the advancement of truth is not today only with the Scientists, or with our Universities and Colleges, neither in Laboratories nor Gardens of Research, but in the Family of God.

We all realize that only where the Family of God, commonly known as the Church, is honored and recognized, and its voice is heard in the counsels of nations, is there any mental, moral, or mechanical growth.

Heathen nations become civilized in the measure that the light of the Revelation of Jesus Christ shines into individual hearts.

The Church then is the depository of the truth.

Hebrews 3:6 says that this house "whose house are we" is His House; we are God's house.

We are members of the blessed Household of the King, sons and daughters of God Almighty.

These mysterious heavenly bodies that swing in their great orbits were created by our Father: they are ours.

This old earth, now under the dominion of Satan, was created in the beginning as our home.

This earth is ours today, though we are kept from our inheritance, but through the Gospel of Jesus Christ and the incoming of eternal life into our spirits, we are conquering some of the lost territory.

The mighty achievements in Electricity, and Aviation, the new powers of Gasoline, discoveries in Chemistry enable us to get our hands once more upon some of the Edenic authority that was lost through the Great Treason.

1 Peter 2:5 tells us that we are a spiritual Household, a holy Priesthood, to offer up spiritual sacrifices, unto God, even the Father through our Lord Jesus Christ.

This is one of the sweetest facts of revelation.

Spiritual sacrifices here mean love sacrifices, heart sacrifices, sacrifices of praise, worship, and love.

This is the holy, inner relationship with our Father.

It is the privilege of every member of the Father's Family to have a little time with Him every day in the Holy of Holies of his own nature, where his spirit fellowships with the Great Father Spirit, a place, where we sit and lean against His breast, look into His face, and draw inspiration from His love and greatness and power, until we finally become imitators of the loving Father in our conduct with men.

Wonderful, wonderful, that we can through Jesus Christ have hourly communication with our busy Father.

In 1 Peter 2:9 we are called the Royal Priesthood.

He says, "But we are an elect race, a royal Priesthood, a holy nation, a people for God's own possession, that we may show forth the excellencies of Him who called you out of darkness into His marvelous light."

This Scripture is a mine of wealth.

It tells us that we are an elect race, and truly we are: born of Heaven, permitted to walk here on earth as revealers of the heart and nature, the purpose and plan, of our Father.

We are a Royal Priesthood: we are connected with the very Throne itself.

We are as near the heart of the Father God as Jesus.

We can talk to Him heart to heart, spirit to spirit, all the time.

As a Royal Priesthood it becomes us to wear the gorgeous garments of Royalty before the beggarly garmented children of the Devil.

We are a holy nation; the word "holy" means separated nation.

We do not belong to the world; we have no part or lot in it.

We belong only to Him, and our business is to tell out by word and deed the glories, the beauties, and wealth of the love and grace of our Father God.

1 Peter 4:17, "For the time is come for judgment to begin at the House of God; and if it begin first at us, what shall be the end of them that obey not the gospel of God?"

Here is one of the most solemn warnings: that God is going to judge His own people and if He does, what will become of the Godless world outside of the Family?

This should stir the heart of every child of God to examine himself carefully that he may escape the judgment when it comes.

Let us walk worthy of our Family, worthy of the traditions of our Great Father God, worthy of such a relationship, worthy of such a Family with such a Father and such a Savior as our Lord Jesus Christ.

The Father God

"For the Father Himself loveth you."

Jesus in this sentence has given us a photograph of the Father's Heart.

It is a Father who loves His children.

It is a Father whose heart is reaching out tenderly toward His own family.

What comfort there is in this precious thought that the Father Himself loves me.

This means that with all the burdens and cares of life the Father Himself loves me.

Whatever the heartache, whatever the burden, whatever the secret grief, the heart of the great Father God yearns over me.

What strength this puts into the soul; what courage to fight the battle when every reason for living has gone and Death would be a relief.

We can take the battle up again and carry it on to victory, because we know that He loves us.

As long as we are loved, and as long as we can love there is a reason for being in the world, but when we cease to love and cease to be the object of love, then the reason for being ends.

Again Jesus tells us that the Father and He will come into our homes and will abide there.

"If a man loves me and keeps my commandments then my Father and I will come unto him and make our abode with him."

This is such a wonderful promise: that the busy God, the hard-working God, the tireless God, He who has charge of every form of life, of every star in the universe, of every blade of grass, of every flower and tree, He whose ear is open to the heart of every human, He who is planning the future for every family will come in and make His home with us.

The heart can hardly take it in; that God and Jesus will come and dwell in our house.

The Emperor of the Universe will dwell in our humble homes.

He who is wisdom itself will put up with our ignorance.

The refined, the Holy One will put up with our coarse selfishness.

It does not seem credible that He will live with us, but He has promised to do it.

This means bearing our burdens, carrying our loads, sharing our poverty, and comforting our hearts.

Oh, what a blessing, what a wonder that this great Father heart, this Omnipotent God will come into our home and help us rear our children, give us wisdom about life's problems, and help us in those dark hours when we know not what to do!

This is Christianity; it is not serving God, but it is a child's living with his Father.

THE ROYAL FAMILY

The family of God is a Royal Family.

God is King of the Universe, and we are His sons and daughters.

We are partakers of His nature.

We are joint heirs with Christ the Lord.

We are called His children.

We are members of the heavenly aristocracy.

Every flower of this earth, every shrub and plant, every rock and mineral, every hidden secret and purpose of God are for us or about us.

The great Father God has only one dream and plan, and this is for His children.

Everything in the entire universe centers in this Family.

We are not poor, weak worms of the dust; we are sons and daughters of God Most High.

> I'm in the Royal Family,
>   My Father God is King;
> The glories of His fellowship
>   Forever let me sing.
> My Father God is King,
>   My Father God is King,
> I'm in the Royal Family,
>   My Father God is King.

How we disown Him and misuse our Royal station by living below our privileges, by seeking the fellowship of man instead of Him, by treating Him as the Secretary of a Charitable Organization where we go when we have used our last resource!

How the Father's heart yearns for us, craves for us. What a blessing He has ready to bestow upon us, what riches are ours to inherit now, what fellowship, what communion in the Royal Family.

God is our Father; We are His children, Sing, Oh, my heart! and rejoice in your wonderful inheritance.

Questions

1. Why is the family fact the basic fact of all scripture?

2. What significance is there in the scripture's calling us God's household?

3. Distinguish between our Holy Priesthood and our Royal Priesthood.

4. Discuss the Father's attitude toward us.

"If ye abide in me, and my words abide in you, ye shall demand your rights and they shall be granted unto you." Jn. 15:7 (Literal translation).

"Verily, verily, I say unto you, He that believeth on me, the works that I do shall he do also; and greater works than these shall he do; because I go unto the Father. And whatsoever ye shall demand in my name, that will I do, that the Father may be glorified in the Son. If ye shall demand anything in my name, that will I do." Jn. 14:12-14.

This scripture does not refer to prayer. It has reference to our using the authority of the name of Jesus to expel the power of disease and demons. Here the Name of Jesus means all to us that the physical presence of Christ could mean. Our demanding anything in that Name brings Him into action.

"For if, through the transgression of the one individual, Death made use of the one individual to seize the sovereignty, all the more shall those who receive God's overflowing grace and gift of righteousness reign as kings in Life through the one individual, Jesus Christ." Rom. 5:17 (Weymouth).

Chapter The Fifteenth

CLAIMING OUR RIGHTS

HRISTIANITY is a legal document. Most of our basic legal terminology comes from the Scripture. The very titles, Old Covenant and New Covenant, are legal terms.

Every step in the plan of Redemption, from the Fall of Man until Jesus Christ was seated at the right hand of the Majesty on High, having redeemed the human race, is simply a series of legal steps perfecting the most remarkable Legal Document the human has in its possession.

The plan of Redemption cannot be understood unless one reads it from the legal point of view.

In this plan of Redemption there are three parties to the contract; God, Man, and Satan.

God must be just to Himself, just to Man, and just to the Devil.

We understand that God created man, placing him here on the earth, and that He conferred upon him certain legal rights. Legal rights that are conferred are more easily forfeited than those that come by nature. These rights man transferred to Satan, God's enemy.

This brings the Devil into the plan so that he must be dealt with, and the whole scheme of Redemption is God's seeking to redeem the human race from Adam's sin, and doing it upon such an equitable basis that it will perfectly satisfy the claims of Justice, meet the needs of man, and defeat Satan on legal grounds.

The Fall of Man was a lawful act; that is, Adam had a legal right to transfer the authority and dominion that God had placed in his hands into the hands of another.

This gives Satan a legal right to rule over man and over creation.

The plan of Redemption is one of the most ingenious, and most wonderful of all the many works of God.

Notice what He is obliged to do.

Man sold himself out to the Devil, making himself a bond slave, and that slavery will last until the lease or period of man's dominion expires.

God must in some way redeem fallen man from his sin, and Satan's dominion.

He must do it in such a way as not to be unjust to Satan, nor unjust to man.

God must recognize and hold inviolate man's treacherous act of transference of dominion.

It was a legal act, and God has no right to arbitrarily annul it.

He must show to Satan perfect justice at all points, and at the same time He must reach man in his helplessness and redeem him.

In order to do this, it is necessary that one come to the earth who is not a subject of Satan, and yet a man, and as a man meet every demand of justice against man.

In order to accomplish this, there must be an Incarnation.

This Incarnate one must not be a subject of Satan, nor a subject of death, and to this end God sends the Holy Spirit to a virgin in Judah, and she conceives and bears a son.

This son is born, not of natural generation but of supernatural.

The child is not a subject of death nor of Satan.

He has the same type of a body that the first man, Adam, had before he sinned.

Every step of the work that was accomplished by this Incarnate One was based upon perfectly legal grounds.

This Incarnate One met the demands, first, of the heart of Deity for a perfect human who would do His will; second, He met the demands of fallen man in that as a man He met the Devil and conquered him in honorable open combat.

"Being tempted in all points, yet without sin."

He goes on the Cross, and God lays upon him the iniquity of the human race.

He, then, with this burden upon Him and under Judgment of God, goes down into Hell and suffers the penalty demanded by Justice.

When He had paid this penalty, He arose from the dead.

He conquered Satan. He broke his dominion and took away his authority and power.

Then, with the trophies of His triumph, He ascended to the right hand of the Majesty on High and laid the tokens of His victory at the feet of His Great Father.

On the ground of this victory, the sinner has a legal right to accept Jesus Christ as a personal Savior.

He has a legal right to Eternal Life.

He has a legal right to Victory over sin and Satan.

He has a legal right to a home in Heaven.

He has a legal right to use the Name of Jesus in prayer.

He has a legal right to his Father's protection and care.

He has a legal right to a son's place in the Family of God.

He has a legal right to the indwelling presence of the Holy Spirit, to the care and protection of the Spirit, and to the intercession and teaching of the Spirit.

He has a legal right to be translated at the Second Coming of the Lord Jesus.

He has a legal right to immortality for the body.

He has a legal right to an inheritance in the New Heavens and New Earth.

He has a legal right to live with his Father throughout Eternity.

Are We Claiming Our Rights?

There is no excuse for the spiritual weakness and poverty of the Family of God when the wealth of Grace and Love of our great Father with His power and wisdom are all at our disposal.

We are not coming to the Father as a tramp coming to the door begging for food; we come as sons not only claiming our legal rights but claiming the natural rights of a child that is begotten in love.

No one can hinder us or question our right of approach to our Father.

When we realize the great need of the unsaved world and know that need can only be met by the great heart of the Father operating through the Church, it stirs us to mighty intercession for a needy world.

God cannot touch the human today except through the Church. It is His only mediator, and if the Church fails to assume its obligation then the hand of God is powerless.

It staggers one to realize that God has limited Himself to our prayer life, and when we refuse to assume the obligations of prayer, God's hands are paralyzed.

Our Authority

"For sin shall not have dominion over you: for ye are not under law, but under grace." Rom. 6:14, or "Sin shall not Lord it over you."

Sin has lost its dominion or authority over us.

Satan has no legal authority over the New Creation, though he has over the old.

Satan has Legal Rights over the sinner that God can not dispute or challenge.

He can sell them as slaves; he owns them, body, soul and spirit.

But the moment we are born again . . . receive Eternal Life, the nature of God, – his legal dominion ends.

Christ is the Legal Head of the New Creation, or Family of God, and all the Authority that was given Him, He has given us: (Matt. 28:18), "All authority in heaven," the seat of authority, and "on earth," the place of execution of authority.

He is "head over all things," the highest authority in the Universe, for the benefit of the Church which is His body.

Eph. 1:20, "Which he wrought in Christ, when he raised him from the dead, and set him at his own right hand in the heavenly places."

Here He is at the "Right Hand of God."

"Far above," that is, His seat of authority transcends all other rulers.

Phil. 2:9-11, "Wherefore also God highly exalted him, and gave unto him the name which is above every name that in the name of Jesus every knee should bow, of things in heaven and things on earth and things under the earth, and that every tongue should confess that Jesus Christ is Lord, to the glory of God the Father."

He has the Name above every name in the three worlds: Heaven, Earth, and Hell.

Every demon and angel is subject to the Imperial Name of Jesus and, wonder of wonders, He gave us the Power of Attorney to use that Name of Might.

All our Authority is based on His Finished Work, but it is all enwrapped in His name.

By His giving us the Legal use of this name He has put omnipotence at our disposal in our combat with Satanic hosts.

Mark 16:17-20, "And these signs shall accompany them that believe: in my name shall they cast out demons; they shall speak with new tongues; they shall take up serpents, and if they drink any deadly thing, it shall in no wise hurt them; they shall lay hands on the sick, and they shall recover.

"So then the Lord Jesus, after he had spoken unto them, was received up into heaven and sat down at the right hand of God.

"And they went forth, and preached everywhere, the Lord working with them, and confirming the word by the signs that followed."

"In my name shall they cast out demons."

Here He defines our Legal Authority.

We shall cast out demons: (this means Authority over demons in their relation to men;) cast them out of peoples' bodies; break their power over those bodies, minds, and spirits; break their power over meetings, homes, and sometimes communities.

Our combat is not against flesh and blood but against the principalities, and powers in heavenly places; or in other words our war is against demons of all ranks, kinds, and authorities.

They are attacking the human everywhere, and especially the children of God.

How are we to defend ourselves against them, or lead an assault on their hosts, and deliver the captives?

The air is pregnant with evil spirits who seek to infest our bodies as bats do old buildings.

The awful power of evil in our land eloquently proves what we write.

"In my Name ye shall speak in new tongues."

This new and startling manifestation of the Spirit is our Legal Right in the Name, where all the mighty powers of God are kept for us.

"In my Name they shall take up serpents, and if they drink any deadly thing it shall not harm them.

"They shall lay hands on the sick, and they shall recover."

Here it is not sufference or pity, but Legal Authority.

You have as much right to demand healing as you have to demand the cashing of a check at a bank where you have a deposit.

You have a Legal Right to deliverance from Satan.

If any one oppresses you or enslaves you in this country, you have a Legal Right to protection from the government to which you belong and pay taxes.

So you have Legal Rights in the Family of God.

No man has a right to hold a white slave today; neither has Satan a Legal Right to hold a child of God in bondage.

All disease is of the Devil.

How glad the Father would be, if we would arise and take our Legal Rights.

All bad habits are of the Devil.

John 14:13-14, 15:16, 16:23-24, "And whatsoever ye shall ask in my name, that will I do, that the Father may be glorified in the Son."

"If ye shall ask anything in my name, that will I do."

This scripture does not refer to prayer as do the others. It is not coming to the Father with a petition, but it is taking the Master's place. It is using His authority to cast out demons, to heal the sick.

A literal translation would read: "If ye shall demand anything in my name, that will I do." In His place we demand sickness and demons to leave in the authority of His Name, and He is there to confirm by His power the word that we speak.

This scripture refers to our using the authority that He gave us in Mark 16:17-18.

Now notice Jn. 16:23-24.

"That whatsoever ye shall ask of the Father in my name, he will give it to you."

"And in that day ye shall ask me nothing.

"Verily, verily, I say unto you, If ye ask anything of the Father, he will give it you in my name.

"Hitherto have ye asked nothing in my name; ask, and ye shall receive, that your joy may be made full."

This is praying to the Father in Jesus' Name.

Here the Mighty Son of God who is now seated in the highest seat of Authority in the Universe gives us the Legal Power of Attorney to use the Might, Authority, and Power of His Name, in our earth struggles against Satan and demons.

In the face of this mighty Fact, poverty and weakness of spirit are criminal.

Here all Heaven with its might and Authority are at our disposal.

It is not trying to have Faith, but knowing the Legal Rights that are yours, as much yours as the clothes you wear — as the bed you sleep on, — the hat you wear, all yours, legally, blessedly yours.

Satan cannot stand before that Name now, any more than he could before the Man who gave you the right to use it, when He walked in Galilee.

Disease is as impotent before it now as it was when its owner, as the Son of Man, walked on earth.

Demons fear it today in the lips of a person who walks with God, as when they bowed before it in Jesus' Day.

All Hell knows the power of that Name; they know our Legal Rights and Authority.

So they are fighting to keep us in ignorance of our Legal Rights; or if we know them, to keep us under condemnation so we will not dare use them.

Matt. 18:18-20, "Verily I say unto you, what things soever ye shall bind on earth shall be bound in heaven; and what things soever ye shall loose on earth shall be loosed in heaven.

"Again I say unto you, that if two of you shall agree on earth as touching anything that they shall ask, it shall be done for them of my Father who is in Heaven.

"For where two or three are gathered together in my name, there am I in the midst of them."

Here the heart stands hushed at its power and God-delegated Authority.

"Whatsoever ye shall bind on earth shall be bound in heaven."

This is unexplored territory to most men today.

We can bind Demons, bind disease, and habits, and bind men so they can not go on in the will of Satan; or use fearsome power to deliver souls over to Satan for the destruction of the body.

"For I verily, being absent in body but present in spirit, have already as though I were present judged him that hath so wrought this thing, in the name of our Lord Jesus, we being gathered together, and my spirit, with power of our Lord Jesus, to deliver such a one unto Satan for the destruction of the Flesh, that the spirit may be saved in the day of Lord Jesus." 1 Cor. 5:3-5.

We may bind the power of Satan over a community, making it easy for men to accept Christ.

"Whatsoever ye shall loose on earth shall be loosed in heaven."

Whatever in Jesus' name we set free, God in Heaven will make good.

What power we have! Let's use it!

Will we arise to our mighty, heaven-given privileges?

Look at the bound men and women everywhere, and the Word challenges us to go out and set the prisoner free.

What does this mean?

All that it says, thank God.

You can set diseased men free. We are doing it daily in our work!

You can set demon-bound men free; you can break the chains that bind men, in that mighty Name.

Most Christians are bound in some manner, either in testimony or in prayer, by fear and devilish doubt; they can be set free by a word if we use that name and then take their privileges.

What bondage to the world, and the binding, devilish spirit of the age we endure, that unseen bondage of the god of this age.

How he holds men in leash!

Yet every spirit may be free, yes, as free as Jesus.

What bondage to the fear of man; yet one authoritative word and the bond shall be broken.

What bondage to fear of want that makes men give pennies instead of dollars; yet there is freedom, glorious freedom for every bondaged soul.

Reader! the Spirit is challenging you to arise and live this Truth.

What prayer meetings we would have if the Christians were free in prayer and testimony!

God's hands are tied until He can use ours.

Angels are our servants.

They cannot do our work. God is limited to our Faith, our obedience.

God is as small in the world as we make Him.

God is big only where some man makes Him big, by using this divinely given authority.

We are the body of Christ; the Head is powerless without our hands and feet.

Oh, men, can't you see how helpless God is until we let Him live omnipotently in our acts?

A sin in the heart binds the arms of God that would embrace a multitude.

Our fear to be used binds God's omnipotence.

Men of God, be God's men and use the authority delegated to you.

How the Early Church Used Their Authority

The Book of Acts is largely our Text Book; it is a series of stories of the triumphs of the Name of Jesus.

The first recorded use of their new heaven conferred authority is given in the third chapter, the healing of the impotent man at the Beautiful Gate.

How quietly and assuredly the apostles say, "In the NAME of Jesus Christ of Nazareth, arise and walk."

How God responds, and the man is healed.

How the city is again moved, how Judaism is shaken!

The apostles are arrested, forbidden to use the Name or preach in it.

That NAME has power in it.

Jesus did no greater miracles when on earth than are recorded in the Book of Acts as done through His Name.

We see Peter striking a man and woman dead for lying. Awful power this is; power to heal and power to slay.

They were walking in the omnipotence of the authority given them by Jesus.

They were taking the words of Jesus seriously.

They were acting as though the Word of God was true.

We have not space to tell of the men who walked in the freshness of this grace of God.

We see Paul cause blindness to come upon the opposers.

We see him cast out demons from Mediums.

We see him stung by a viper and no harm come.

We see the sick healed, the dead raised.

Whole heathen cities turn toward the unknown God of the Jews.

In thirty-three short years this gospel, backed by the power of the Name, in the hands of common men was carried into every part of the Roman World.

We see aprons, handkerchiefs, touched by Paul, sent out and laid on the sick, do the same mighty acts that Paul did in person.

These men lived in bodies like ours, with passions like ours, made mistakes as we do; yet they wrought miracles by this God-inspired authority over demons and disease.

They were just men of like passions with us.

What ails us, why do we not walk in power instead of weakness?

Paul could deliver a man over unto Satan for destruction of his body, or as he did Hymeneus and Alexander, that they might be taught not to blaspheme. (1 Tim. 1:20.)

"Of whom is Hymeneus and Alexander whom I delivered unto Satan, that they might be taught not to blaspheme."

Preachers were dangerous in those days.

Christians had power to prove their claims.

They preached; they practiced. They made good.

"They delivered the goods," as men say today.

Their Faith stood not in word only, but in demonstration and power.

Miracles were the common order of the day.

Christianity was a miracle in their day.

Personal Experience and Observation

The writer has seen hundreds healed, soreness from sprains leave while prayer was being offered, swelling reduced instantly, ruptures healed like a flash from glory, and consumption in last stages healed, all soreness and coughing leaving at once, broken backs instantly healed, cancers instantly healed.

Space forbids giving individual cases.

But the authority invested in the Name is as mighty now as in Paul's day.

We have seen demons cast out, men and women set free, testimonies restored, power in prayer given.

We have seen the insane set free instantly.

We have seen whole communities put under the conviction of the Holy Spirit, so that great fear was in them all.

We have seen other places set free from Satanic bondage.

We have seen God set many free from fear and avarice.

We have seen souls in bondage to habits given liberty in a single instant.

We have seen the drunkard freed from bondage and arise free while we were praying.

Yes, we have Legal Rights, Legal Authority; let us live in it.

Questions

1. In the plan of Redemption, who are the three parties involved in the contract?

2. Name five legal rights that belong to every man as a result of Redemption in Christ.

3. Why is it that if the Church fails the hand of God is powerless?

4. What are the two ways in which the name of Jesus may be used?

5. What should the name of Jesus mean to you?

"Knowing this, that our old man was crucified with him, that the body of sin might be done away, and so we should no longer be in bondage to sin; for he that hath died is justified from sin." "Even so reckon ye also yourselves to be dead unto sin, but alive unto God in Christ Jesus.

"Let not sin therefore reign in your mortal body, that ye should obey the lusts thereof: neither present your members unto sin as instruments of unrighteousness; but present yourselves unto God, as alive from the dead, and your members as instruments of righteousness unto God. For sin shall not have dominion over you: for ye are not under law, but under grace." Rom. 6:6, 7, 11-14.

"I beseech you therefore, brethren, by the mercies of God, to present your bodies a living sacrifice, holy, acceptable to God, which is your spiritual service. And be not fashioned according to this world; but be ye transformed by the renewing of your mind, that ye may prove what is the good and acceptable and perfect will of God." Rom. 12:1-2.

Chapter The Sixteenth

GOD WANTS TRANSFIGURED BODIES

BESEECH you therefore, Brethren,, by the mercies of God, to present your bodies, a living sacrifice, holy, acceptable unto God, which is your reasonable service." This is truly a most revolutionary teaching.

All through the Epistles, Paul has been urging with mighty argument and appeal and warning for us to submit our souls and spirits to the will of God, the Father.

Now he turns his mighty logic of appeal toward our bodies.

Why is it that He should care anything about our bodies that are to perish?

The secret lies here: our soul and our spirit are both tremendously influenced by the habits of our physical body.

No man can live in sweet fellowship with the Father with unclean physical habits, for sooner or later these habits defile the soul, bind the spirit in bondage, and break its fellowship with its great Father God.

If the spirit goes unwillingly into paths that the body insists upon going in, sooner or later there is war between the body and the spirit, and the spirit usually loses the fight.

Paul asks that our bodies be living sacrifices.

The Jewish sacrifice was dead.

He asks now that our bodies shall be fragrant, living offerings ascending up, that this body of ours shall not only be a free-will offering, a living sacrifice, but that it shall be a holy one, a fragrant one.

This is a heart-searching appeal, asking that these bodies of ours be holy, separated from every known sin, and cleansed by our own conduct.

The blood of Jesus Christ cleanses our spirits, but we must cleanse our mind, will, and heart from evil thoughts, and our bodies from unclean habits by His grace.

The Holy Spirit can not keep unclean and impure thoughts out of our minds unless we will to have them kept out.

The Holy Spirit can not cleanse our body of dirty, evil habits unless we cooperate with Him.

How fitting it is that the temple in which the renewed spirit dwells should be a holy temple, pure, swept, and cleansed.

He asks not only for a holy body but also for a well-pleasing body for presentation unto God.

The word "acceptable" really means well-pleasing, and he says, "This is our spiritual service," or worship; "a service belonging to reason" would be a literal rendering. It would not be reasonable to expect that God was going to dwell in a filthy, dirty temple.

He wants His temple kept clean.

He wants a clean, sweet, wholesome place in which to dwell.

And then Paul continues, "Be not fashioned according to this age in which you are living, but be ye transfigured by the renewing of your mind, then you will be able to prove what is that good, acceptable and perfect will of God."

I question if any one with a body filled with unclean habits will ever know the will of God.

OUR BODIES AND SINS

The problem of victory over sin has caused more trouble in the individual life of the believer than any other one problem.

Those who teach the Second Work of Grace have tried to solve it and have bitterly failed.

The Dual Nature teachers tried their hand at it but made no better success.

Paul has given us a clear message in regard to it.

In the Book of Romans after he has dealt with our spirits and told us how to get in right relationship with God, then in Chapter 6, verses 12-14, he begins to deal with this problem.

Notice what he says, "Let not sin therefore reign in your mortal body, that ye should obey the lusts thereof; neither present your members unto sin as instruments of unrighteousness; but present yourselves unto God, as alive from the dead, and your members as instruments of righteousness unto God. For sin shall not have dominion over you for ye are not under the law, but under grace."

Sin operates almost altogether through the members of our bodies.

By "members" Paul and Jesus and James mean the tongue, the eyes, the ears, the hands, the feet, and the other organs of our bodies.

Practically all the sins ever committed have been committed through some of these organs, or these members of the body.

Jesus told us in His Sermon on the Mount that it were better to pluck our eye out, than have it cause our whole body to be cast into the Lake of Fire, that it was better to cut our right hand off than have that cause our whole body to be cast into the Lake of Fire.

James tells us that the tongue is a little member set on fire by Hell which will start a conflagration that no fire company will be able to control.

Notice in this Scripture, "Let not sin reign in your mortal body," literally, let not sin reign as king in that death-doomed body of yours that you obey its lusts.

Before accepting Christ you had evil habits. You said things, sang things, told things with your mouth which, if you repeat them now, will break your fellowship with the Father.

You ate and drank things that if you eat or drink now will perhaps destroy your spiritual life.

You may have had other bad habits, but those must be discontinued; the deeds of the past must be slain.

In Romans 8:13 "If ye put to death the deeds of the body, ye shall live" then in right relationship to God.

The body itself is not wrong; there is no evil in it. It is only that you submit it to practices that are wrong.

There are other members of the body; the hands and feet that must not touch things, nor handle things, nor lead you where it will injure your spiritual life.

"Being made free from sin, ye became servants of righteousness. I speak after the manner of men because of the infirmity of your flesh: for as ye presented your members as servants to uncleanness and to iniquity, even so now present your members as servants to righteousness unto sanctification." Rom. 6:18.

The one who can keep the body under, rule it, will be able to live a life well-pleasing to the Father in unbroken fellowship; but if one permits the body to sin against the spirit, the Devil rules his life.

Clean your hands and your dreams. Allow nothing in your heart life that will in any wise tarnish the spirit and break your fellowship and joy, full of the wealth of Heaven.

The problem of sanctification in the New Testament is a problem of the body.

In nearly every Scripture where the word sanctification or holiness is used, it is in connection with the physical body.

1 Thessalonians 4:3-8, "For this is the will of God, even your sanctification, that ye abstain from fornication; that each one of you know how to possess himself of his own vessel in sanctification and honor, not in the passion of lust, even as the Gentiles who know not God; that no man transgress, and wrong his brother in the matter because the Lord is an avenger in all these things, as also we fore-warned you and testified.

"For God called us not for uncleanness, but in sanctification."

You notice here that it is a setting apart of our physical body to holy use, and the word is used in the same sense in the 6th Chapter of Romans.

You remember that the Greek words for holiness and sanctification come from the same root, "separate or set apart." Just as the Temple was set apart for the worship of Jehovah so now our bodies, indwelt by the Holy Spirit, are set apart, sanctified completely unto the Lord.

Questions

1. Why does He want us to present our bodies to Him as living sacrifices?

2. Explain the influence of bodily habits over the spirit and soul.

3. Explain Romans 6:12.

"Shall this body, this curious workmanship of Heaven, so wonderfully and fearfully made, always lie in ruins and never be repaired. This we know that 'it is not a thing impossible with God to raise the dead.' He that could first form our bodies out of nothing, is certainly able to form them anew and repair the wastes of time.

"The omniscient God knows how to collect, distinguish, and compound all those scattered and mingled seeds of our mortal bodies. Matter we know is capable of prodigious alterations and refinements; and there it will appear in the highest perfection. The bodies of the saints will be formed glorious, incorruptible, without the seeds of sickness or death. The glorified body of Christ, which is undoubtedly matter carried to the highest perfection that matter is capable of, will be the pattern after which they shall be formed.

"Then will the body be able to bear up under the exceeding great and eternal weight of glory; it will no longer be a clog or incumbrance to the soul, but a proper instrument and assistant in all the exalted services and enjoyments of the heavenly state."

— SAMUEL DAVIS.

Chapter The Seventeenth

MORTALITY AND IMMORTALITY

HEN God created man, He created him to be His eternal companion.

Man, as stated in Eccles. 3:11, "has eternity set in his heart;" in other words, man is an eternal being; he belongs to God's class.

Man does not belong to the animal creation, for the animal belongs to time, but man, to eternity.

When man was created, he was made a perfect human being. His body was eternal.

It would seem as though God's original scheme was for man to live eternally as a physical being.

Physiologists tell us that the human body has the power of renewing itself every seven years, and some of our latest scientists tell us that they see no reason for man's not living eternally in his physical body, that they can see no reason for death's slaying him.

All the plans of the New Heavens and the New Earth are for man with his physical body that will live eternally.

When man was first created he was not mortal, neither was he immortal.

The word "Mortal" in both the Hebrew and the Greek means subject to death, frail, limited; in other words, a subject of the Devil, for death did not come to man until he became a subject of Satan.

The moment that he committed treason and became Satan's subject, Satan breathed into him his own nature, and man died in spirit; this is the primal basic death.

Then this spiritual death began to operate upon his physical body, and it took nearly a thousand years before it could bring physical death or dissolution. It eventually succeeded, and Adam died at the age of nine hundred and thirty odd years.

It took several thousand years to bring the span of life below a hundred years.

Adam, at the beginning, was not a subject of death; death had no dominion over him whatever.

Just as water, although contaminated, has the power of purifying itself, so man physically had the power of rejuvenation, of physical recreation so that he would have eternally existed in the body; but when he sinned he instantly became mortal, subject to Satan, and subject to death.

Perhaps one of the most striking facts in this connection is the name Adam gave to his first grandchild.

According to Genesis 5:6 he named that child Enosh, which literally means mortal, frail, Satan-ruled.

How Adam's sin and treason must have clung to his memory!

How it must have overwhelmed every other thing in his mind to have caused him to name his first grandchild, "Mortal!"

The blood of Abel was still crimsoning his memory.

His awful sin in the garden haunted him day and night.

Immortality is something that comes to the Believer, and to the Believer only at the Second Coming of the Lord Jesus.

The word "Immortal" is never applied to the soul as heathen writers have used it.

Men often speak of our "immortal soul;" our soul is neither mortal nor immortal.

Our souls are eternal.

It is our bodies that today are mortal, but if we have received eternal life, at the Second Coming of the Lord Jesus, we shall receive immortality for our bodies.

Adam was not mortal, neither was he immortal; he was a perfect human.

Jesus had the same kind of a physical body that Adam had.

He was not conceived of natural generation, so He did not partake of mortality from His mother.

They could not kill Jesus until He became our sin substitute.

He says in John 10:18, "I have power to lay down my life and power to take it up again; no one can take it from me."

That authority had been given Him by His Father.

When Jesus suffered upon the Cross, the Father took our sin nature, spiritual death, and laid it upon the spirit of His Son.

The moment He did this, Jesus became mortal, subject to death, subject to Satan.

This point has been taken up at greater length in another chapter.

When Jesus arose from the dead, immortality was given to His body, and He took that body with Him up into Heaven. Today He is seated at the right hand of the Majesty on High with an Immortal physical body, the same kind that we are going to have when He returns.

Resurrection

The resurrection of the human body and its immortality are perfectly natural as well as inevitable as can be seen when one understands the Plan of Redemption.

Man has no desire to be a disembodied spirit floating through space; he wants his physical body, eternally.

He has been connected with the physical body, and when you take the physical body away you have robbed him of the first asset of life.

Not only Jesus but also the writers of the Epistles spoke clearly of the resurrection of our physical bodies.

As Jesus was raised, so we shall be raised.

Jesus has an immortal body, and we shall have an immortal body. We shall have ours at His return.

It is not only an immortal body but it is our own body. If it were not so it would not be a resurrection but a new creation.

We shall recognize each other and enjoy the same things we have enjoyed here in the physical condition.

Only perfect bodies will enter into the perfect Eternal Existence in the New Heavens and the New Earth.

To deny a resurrection means to deny the very Plan of Redemption.

Paul declares that this mortal will put on immortality and this corruptible put on incorruption: "so also is the resurrection of the dead. It is sown in corruption; it is raised in incorruption; it is sown in dishonor, it is raised in glory; it is sown in weakness; it is raised in power; it is sown in the natural body; it is raised a spiritual body. If there is a natural body, there is a spiritual body." 1 Cor. 15:42-44.

He tells us "we all shall not sleep, but we shall all be changed, in a moment, in the twinkling of an eye, at the last trump; for the trumpet shall sound and the dead shall be raised incorruptible, and we shall be changed." Verses 51, 52.

This is the climax of everything in the entire Plan of redemption, and to deny the climax is to reduce the whole plan to the scrap heap.

We are to be raised; these physical bodies of ours shall be inhabited by ourselves.

Man is himself a spirit, but he dwells in a physical body.

He has an intellect through which he thinks, sensibilities through which he feels, a will through which he chooses and selects, and a spirit through which he loves God.

It is evident that one day the bodies of our loved ones shall be raised from the dead and that they themselves shall return from heaven, as it tells us in Thessalonians, to "be clothed upon" with these raised bodies, and then enter the unexplored realities of the New Heavens and the New Earth.

THE NEW HEAVEN AND THE NEW EARTH

The universal man has a tradition of a golden age when there was no sin nor death to mar the earth or the human race, when man and God walked together in happy fellowship.

It has another dream of a golden age that is to come when death will be no more, and sin, pain, hatred, and sorrow shall be not even a dream.

The North American Indian calls it his Happy Hunting-Ground.

Every language has its own name for it; it is the universal demand of the human.

The most degraded of earth's millions have a hope of a New Heaven and a New Earth; although it may be grotesque, nevertheless the hope, the dream is there.

The Scriptures clearly teach of the glory of man at the beginning of the world without sin, without death, without the curse; of the time when love ruled over the animal and the human kingdoms.

We have the story that tells us that through man's treason sin came and Death began her fearful dominion of devastation, but the Scriptures point with unerring clearness to another golden age where sin can never come, where death and pain and tears will never intrude.

Paul tells us in Romans 8 that the earnest expectation of the creation waits for the revelation of the sons of God, for the creation was subject to vanity (that is to the Devil) not of its own will but by reason of him (that is, Adam) who subjected it. However, creation has hope of deliverance from the bondage of corruption into the liberty of the glory of the children of God, for we know that the whole creation groans and travails in pain together even until now.

It is waiting for the coming of the Lord Jesus when the long humiliated Church shall suddenly come into her own.

Satan shall be bound and cast into his prison house, his long dominion over, and the sons and daughters of God burst forth into glory with their immortal bodies, into the never ending ages of a glorious Eternity.

John tells us in Revelation that when Death, the last enemy is cast into the Lake of Fire, then will come forth the New Heaven and the New Earth and the first heaven and the first earth shall pass and the sea shall be no more.

God will never permit to come into our New Heaven one star or planet to remind us of the old sin, and heartaches of this age. He even says that the "sea shall be no more;" it shall not remind us of the death of loved ones who have sunk beneath its pitiless waves.

He shall wipe away all tears, and there shall be no more crying, nor pains, nothing to remind us of the old life. These things shall pass away, and He will make all things new, and the Church will then enter into its vast inheritance.

Paul tells us in Ephesians that in the days to come the Great Father God is going to give us the wealth and riches that He has stored up in His great love during the Eternity of the past for us.

Oh, the glorious truth of the wealth, the riches, the joy that belongs to God's family!

Through the ages of the ages we are going to know one another, talk with one another, enjoy heavenly bliss eternally.

There will be light without our old sun, because darkness would remind us of the sin life of the past; there will be one Eternal Day with no fatigue, no sorrow, and no pain.

Blessed be the hope of the New Heaven and the New Earth.

‡   ‡   ‡

Questions

1. Why was man given an eternal body at creation?

2. What does the word "mortal" mean? When did man's body become mortal?

3. What type of a body did Christ have?

4. When will the believer receive immortality for his body?

5. What does God reveal to us about the New Heaven and the New Earth?

"The declaration that in the Gospel there is a revelation of the righteousness of God does not mean that the Gospel has revealed the fact that God was righteous. That revelation antedated the Gospel. The declaration clearly means that the Gospel reveals the fact that God places Righteousness at the disposal of men who in themselves are unrighteous. — If you tell me that Salvation is deliverance from Hell, I tell you that you have an utterly inadequate understanding of what Salvation is. If you tell me that Salvation is forgiveness of sins, I shall affirm that you have not a very practical understanding of what salvation is. Unless there be more in salvation than deliverance from penalty and forgiveness of sins committeed, then I solemnly say that salvation cannot satisfy my own heart and conscience. Man may not obey it, but there in the deeps of human conscience there is a response to righteousness, an admission of its call, of its beauty, its necessity. Salvation, then, is the making possible of that righteousness." — GEORGE CAMPBELL MORGAN.

Chapter The Eighteenth

RIGHTEOUSNESS

E HAVE seen through this study that the reason for man was the heart hunger of God for fellowship. This fellowship between God and man was destroyed by the entrance of spiritual death into man's spirit.

Spiritual death alienated man from God. Man felt immediately after his treason his inability to stand in God's presence uncondemned.

A sin consciousness, a sense of unworthiness, and an inferiority complex were the products of spiritual death that ruled his life. Fellowship between God and man had been made impossible.

The reason for man's redemption was the same as the reason for his creation — God's desire for Fellowship.

If man was to be restored to perfect fellowship with the Father-God, righteousness must be given to him. All sin consciousness, sense of unworthiness, and inferiority must be eliminated from man's spirit and mind.

Therefore, the first problem that the Father faced ·in providing man's redemption was that of providing righteousness for him. Righteousness may be defined as the following: The ability to stand in the presence of God without the sense of sin, guilt, or inferiority.

Unless man is given the ability to stand in God's presence as he did before the fall, perfect fellowship between God and man cannot be attained. Unless the consciousness of sin that was once man's is eradicated, man's fellowship with the Father cannot be spontaneous and free.

Let me state it again: The reason for the New Creation is that the fellowship between God and man might be restored. If that fellowship cannot be based upon the grounds of man's being made righteous, redemption will have failed to accomplish its purpose. For as long as man has a consciousness of sin, a sense of unworthiness in the presence of his own Father, there can be no joyous fellowship between them.

If God cannot make man righteous and as free from a sin consciousness and condemnation as he was before sin entered the world, then Satan's work in Adam has been more effectual than God's work in Christ. If God cannot destroy the sin consciousness and sense of unworthiness and weakness in man (all products of spiritual death), then Christ has not destroyed the works of Satan, and the imprints of spiritual death are still upon man's consciousness, marring his fellowship with the Father.

As we study the subject of Righteousness the teachings and traditions of man cannot be authoritative to us. The Word alone must be our authority. Let us study the scriptures to find out what God has made known to us about righteousness.

The Father-God realized that Righteousness must be given to man upon legal grounds. This was the major problem that He faced in redemption.

It is expressed in Romans 3:26: "For the showing, I say, of his righteousness at this present season: that he might himself be righteous and the righteousness of him that hath faith in Jesus." (Revised Version.)

If He is to have perfect fellowship with man, He must make man as righteous as Himself. This is the problem that He reveals in this scripture: That he might become the righteousness of the one who has faith in Christ. If He is to become the righteousness of the one who has faith in Christ, that one will become as righteous as Himself.

He must become the righteousness of the one who accepts this redemption in Christ, and yet He must be just in so doing. In other words, it must be enacted upon grounds of justice.

The scriptures not only reveal the problem of righteousness as the major problem that God faced in redemption but also as the heart of the gospel message that is given to the world. In fact, the gospel is a revelation of righteousness.

In writing to the Romans, Paul expresses his desire to visit them that he might bring to them the revelation of the gospel given to him. He gives the thesis of that gospel to them in Roman 1:16-17: "For I am not ashamed of the gospel: for it is the power of God unto salvation to everyone that believeth; to the Jew first, and also to the Greek. For therein is revealed a righteousness of God from faith unto faith: as it is written, but the righteous shall live by faith."

God's redemption has been adequate and sufficient to meet the needs of man, and the Gospel is a revelation of the righteousness that He has made available to man: for therein is revealed a righteousness of God that becomes man's on the basis of faith alone.

Romans the fourth chapter and the twenty-fifth verse reveals to us how God has provided that righteousness upon legal grounds: "Who was delivered up for our trespasses, and was raised for our justification." A literal translation reads: "Who was delivered up for our trespasses, and was raised when we were declared righteous."

Roman 5:19 throws light upon this scripture: "For as through the one man's disobedience the many were made sinners even so through the obedience of the one shall the many be made righteous."

Redemption is based upon a two-fold law: Man's identification with Adam, and man's identification with Christ. It is through the identification of humanity with one man, Adam, that all were made sinners, that is, all came under condemnation. It is therefore reasonable that through one man all be made righteous, as the human race was identified with Christ when He paid the penalty of that transgression. Notice the scripture: "Who was delivered up for our trespasses."

Christ was delivered up, crucified, because He had been made one with us. Our spiritual death was laid upon Him, and He was made to become sin, (2 Cor. 5:17). (This has already been covered fully in a previous chapter entitled The Sin-Bearer.)

Now notice this tremendous fact: He was raised when we were declared righteous. Because He had been made all that spiritual death had made us, He could not be raised from that condition until man had been declared righteous. When the claims of justice against the human race were satisfied, Christ could be raised. 1 Timothy 3:16 reveals that Christ Himself was made righteous in spirit. He had been made sin, and when the penalty was paid He, Himself, had to be made righteous.

Therefore, when Christ arose from the dead the human race had legally been declared righteous. The human race stood legally before God as free from sin as if Adam had not sinned.

Notice 2 Cor. 5:18-20 "But all things are of God, who reconciled us to himself through Christ, and gave unto us the ministry of reconciliation; To wit, that God was in Christ reconciling the world unto himself, not reckoning unto them their trespasses."

Redemption is all of God who has reconciled the world unto Himself. Because of the reconciliation, He is not reckoning unto them their trespasses. He is not holding against them an account of their sins. However, we do not want to overlook the following fact: Although man has legally been declared righteous in Christ, it is only his personal acceptance of the reconciliation in Christ that will save him. He will be convicted of only one sin, his rejection of Jesus Christ as his Savior.

Man's being legally declared righteous in Christ made it possible for him to approach God through Christ to receive eternal life, God's nature. This is the second step in this revelation of righteousness. First, we were declared righteous, that is, freed from the condemnation wrought by Adam's transgression. Second, when we accept Christ as Savior and Lord we become freed from all personal transgressions, and we have imparted to us God's nature.

Receiving God's nature is in reality receiving His righteousness. It was Christ's having our spiritual death laid upon Him that made Him sin, as unrighteous as we were. Now our receiving God's nature causes us to become His righteousness. 2 Cor. 5:21 reveals this fact: "Him who knew no sin He made to become sin on our behalf; that we might become the righteousness of God in Him" He became sin by receiving our nature; we become the righteousness of God by receiving His nature.

Then, to further reveal to us our righteousness in Christ, He gives us 1 Cor. 1:30 "But of him are ye in Christ Jesus, who was made unto us wisdom from God, and righteousness, and sanctification, and redemption." Christ, Himself, is the righteousness of the child of God. That gives him the same standing before the Father that Christ has.

No wonder He calls the gospel a revelation of righteousness. When Christ arose from the dead, we had been declared righteous legally. When we were born again, we became the righteousness of God, and Christ, Himself, is our righteousness.

This is the one message that God has tried to make clear to our hearts that we might be free from the sin consciousness that was ours as a result of spiritual death, that we might joyfully take our place in His family as His sons and daughters, and that we might walk as fearlessly in the presence of sin, demons, disease, and circumstances as did Christ, Himself.

This message of Righteousness is the one message that Satan has hindered our knowing. To us the gospel has been a revelation of sin. We have preached sin to the unsaved man, and sins to the Christian, producing weakness and unstableness.

Satan has made us think that it was a mark of humility before God to boast of our sinful and weak and unworthy condition. It is not humility, however, to speak of ourselves as poor, weak worms of the dust. It is dishonoring God, dishonoring redemption and the blood of Jesus Christ. It is considering Satan's work in Adam more effectual than redemption in Christ.

We can understand why Satan has hindered our knowing the righteousness that is ours.

As far as the New Creation is concerned Satan has been brought to naught, Heb. 2:14: "Since then the children are sharers in flesh and blood he also himself in like manner partook of the same; that through death he might bring to naught him that had the authority of death, that is the Devil. And might deliver all them who through fear of death were all their lifetime subject to bondage." Satan has no right to rule the New Creation. In the Name of Jesus Christ we have authority over him. Therefore, if the body of Christ down through the ages had taken its place as the actual righteousness of God and stood fearlessly in the presence of Satan and all his hosts, the power of Satan would have been broken in a large measure over the human race. But Satan has made the church so conscious of sin and unworthiness that in his presence they have felt too weak to break his power or to live free from his dominion.

Can you not see what this message of Righteousness will mean in your life? It will solve every problem that you have. Your fellowship with the Father will be sweet and joyous, without a sense of condemnation, with nothing to stand between you and Him. It will not be hard to trust God for your needs. You will have confidence in your own prayer life and your testimony.

224 of His Family

You will gain a reputation for having your prayers answered, because you will know that when you ask in His Name that He hears you, and that if He hears you you have the petition you desire. You will be able to pray for the sick in the authority of the Name of Jesus Christ because you will not feel too unworthy to use it.

Here is the secret of the power that you have been seeking in your life. It is in knowing that you are the righteousness of God. No longer will you be hindered in taking your place or using the authority of the Name of Jesus through which He will be glorified.

‡   ‡   ‡

Questions

1. What was the first problem that the Father-God faced in providing a Redemption for man?

2. Why can there be no perfect fellowship between God and man if righteousness is not restored to man?

3. Upon what grounds has God made it possible for man to become His righteousness?

4. Why has Satan hindered our knowing that we are the actual righteousness of God?

5. What does this message of Righteousness mean to you?

Chapter The Nineteenth

FELLOWSHIP

IN THE early days of my ministry I wondered why the largest percentage of church members and those whom I had led to Christ myself were spiritual failures. I wondered if after all, Christianity was a bag of holes. I was very zealous. I had consecration services every week. I preached hard and worked hard, but my people failed to attend prayer meetings despite all that I could do.

Years went by. One day I was preaching in a city near Boston. A Bible teacher whom I had noticed in the audience said to me, "I see you make a distinction between union and communion," or Relationship and Fellowship.

I found that I had been preaching something that I had not analyzed carefully. I rushed to my room and began to look up the subject of Fellowship.

At last I arrived. I discovered that the word "Backslide" did not occur in the New Testament. It was a word that dealt with servants.

But the word "Fellowship" concerned the sons and daughters of God.

1 Cor. 1:9 "God is faithful, through whom ye were called into the fellowship of His Son Jesus Christ, our Lord."

We were called out of the discord, bitterness, and unhappiness of Spiritual Death into Fellowship with the Great Father-God of the Universe. Then I saw that Fellowship was the heart reason for Creation. God wanted Fellowship with human beings, and so He created the Universe. When man fell and that Fellowship was broken, the reason for Redemption was the restoration of that lost Fellowship.

The heart secret of the New Creation is Fellowship. God could not Fellowship with the old creation that was ruled by the adversary, so He recreated it, imparted to it His own nature so that there could be a perfect Fellowship.

I found that the secret of prayer, really meeting the Father face to face, lies in the word Fellowship.

The secret of getting into the Word, knowing it, having it abide in us in power, lies in Fellowship. The secret of preaching so that it will awaken men, cause them to turn to the Lord, lies in Fellowship. The secret of joy, a vibrant rich spiritual life, is Fellowship.

Broken Fellowship in families spells misery and danger. If it is not remedied it will cause divorce and a broken home.

The same law works in the spiritual life. Every step out of love means broken Fellowship and sooner or later, spiritual wreckage unless the Fellowship is restored.

The spiritual condition of our church today is a result of broken Fellowship. It is the tragedy of the church.

The first epistle of John teaches the sacredness and beauty of Fellowship and the danger of broken Fellowship.

1 Jn. 1:3 "That which we have seen and heard declare we unto you also, that ye also may have fellowship with us: yea, and our fellowship is with the Father, and with His Son Jesus Christ."

1 Jn. 1:5 Tells us that "God is light and in Him is no darkness at all. If we say we have Fellowship with Him and walk in the darkness, we lie, and do not the truth."

Here is the contrast: God is Light and when I walk in the light, I walk in Fellowship; when I step out of Light, out of love, I step into Darkness.

1 Jn. 2:10, 11 "He that loveth his brother abideth in the light, and there is no occasion of stumbling in him. But he that hateth his brother is in the darkness, and walketh in the darkness, and knoweth not whither he goeth, because the darkness hath blinded his eyes." The darkness is broken Fellowship.

How to Restore Broken Fellowship

1 Jn. 1:9 "If we confess our sins, He is faithful and Righteous to forgive us our sins, and to cleanse us from all unrighteousness."

In the next verse he says if we say we have not sinned, and yet we are out of Fellowship, we are liars.

Broken Fellowship can be restored the moment we confess our sins. God is faithful and forgives us. The broken Fellowship is a thing of the past. As surely as you confess your sins He forgives. What He forgives He forgets. There is no memory of it. We should never remember it again. We should go on as though the Fellowship had never been broken.

1 Jn. 2:1-2 "My little children these things write I unto you that ye may not sin. (But) if any man sin, we have an Advocate with the Father, Jesus Christ the Righteous."

First you notice, you have an Advocate, a Lawyer, with the Father and if you do sin, that lawyer will take up your case the moment you ask forgiveness. You may fear that you are not Righteous and cannot stand in the Father's presence but Jesus is the Righteous One. He can go into the Father's presence and plead your case and restore your broken Fellowship.

We cannot have revivals with Broken Fellowship. We cannot have power with God or power with men if we have broken Fellowship. It is very easy to have Fellowship restored. It is very dangerous to live in darkness, for we know not whither we are going.

‡ ‡ ‡

Questions

1. To whom does the word "Backslide" refer?

2. Whom does the word "Fellowship" concern?

3. Why is the heart secret of the New Creation fellowship?

4. Discuss the importance of maintaining our fellowship with the Father.

5. How may broken fellowship be restored?

Chapter The Twentieth

HOW TO BECOME A CHRISTIAN

"I HAVE tried to become a Christian so many times and failed, that I have lost faith."

"In what have you lost faith?"

"I suppose I have lost faith in myself. You see I have wanted to be a Christian, I have wanted to have God's help in this fight of life. I have gone to the altar again and again, and received nothing. I've sought and cried after God so many times and failed."

"Did you ever realize that salvation is a gift, that it is not necessary that you go any place to get it? You can find it anywhere. Did you ever realize that it is not what you do, but what He did for you that counts? All there is to receiving Eternal Life, becoming a child of God is to receive something instead of giving something. You have tried to get it by earning it.

"It is a gift from the Father's heart to you. Most of us have thought that it was giving up, surrendering and confessing our sins. It is not.

"It is receiving Jesus Christ as your Savior and confessing Him as your Lord."

IT IS SO SIMPLE

"It can't be as easy as that. I have always heard that one must DO and GIVE UP a lot of things."

"No, there is nothing in the Scripture that tells us that. Turn with me, if you will, to Isa. 53:6.

" 'All we like sheep have gone astray; we have turned everyone to his own way; and Jehovah hath laid on Him the iniquity of us all.'

"He is describing you. You have turned to your own way. We have been stubborn and willful and yet He laid upon Christ, the iniquity of us all. You notice in this that you did not do a thing to save yourself or to help yourself.

"God laid on Jesus your sins. Yes, He laid you upon Him. This requires nothing on your part, does it?

"Notice the next Scripture, John 1:12, 'But as many as received Him, to them gave He the right to become children of God, even to them that believe on His Name.'

"Here you do nothing except to receive Christ as God's gift.

"Notice another Scripture, John 3:16, 'God so loved the world, that He gave His only begotten Son, that whosoever believeth on Him should not perish, but have Eternal Life.'

"This is the Father giving His Son as your substitute, as your Savior and all He asks for you to do is to accept that Son as your Savior. He does not ask you to do a single thing but to believe, and believing means acting on His Word.

"Rom. 4:25 says, 'Who was delivered up on account of our trespasses and was raised when we were Justified, or declared Righteous.'

"God delivered Him up on our behalf and He was raised when He had paid the penalty of our transgressions. All we do is to accept what He did.

THE PRICE IS PAID

"In the next verse it says, 'Being therefore Justified on the ground of faith, we have peace with God.'

"You have nothing to do yet, have you? It has all been done for you. All you have to do is to accept it.

"Rom. 10:9-11 declares, "That if thou shalt confess with thy mouth Jesus as Lord, and shalt believe in thy heart that God raised Him from the dead, thou shalt be saved: for with the heart man believeth unto Righteousness; and with the mouth confession is made unto salvation. For the scripture saith, Whosoever believeth on Him shall not be put to shame.'

"Let us look at these verses carefully. 'That if thou shalt confess with thy mouth, Jesus as Lord." That will be the end of your going your own way and doing your own will. That isn't hard because your own way has not been a happy way, and it has not been a successful way. It has been a way of hardship, loneliness without God.

"Now He says He wants you to change from being the Lord of your own life or yielding to the lordship of your enemy, and confess with your lips Jesus as Lord."

"That is easy to do. I'm glad to confess Jesus as Lord. I do know that God raised Him from the dead."

"Then what does the Word say?"

"That I shall be saved."

"When will you be saved?"

"When I believe."

"Do you believe now?"

"I do."

"I never dreamed it could be that easy. Do you mean that I am Born Again now?"

"1 Jn. 5:1 declares 'Whosoever believeth that Jesus is the Christ, is begotten of God.' Do you believe that Jesus is the Christ?"

"Certainly I do."

"What are you?"

"Does that mean I am a child of God now?"

"1 Jn. 3:2 says, 'Beloved, now are we children of God, and it is not yet made manifest what we shall be.' When are you a child of God?"

"Now."

"How do you know you are? How do you know you are born of God?"

THE WORD IS OUR EVIDENCE

"Because the Word says I am. I took Jesus as my Savior. I confessed Him as my Lord. I must be His child. The Word declares I am. What about receiving Eternal Life?"

"1 Jn. 5:13, 'These things have I written unto you, that ye may know that ye HAVE Eternal Life, even unto you that believe on the name of the Son of God.' Do you believe on the Name of Jesus?"

"I certainly do."

"Then what have you?"

"I have Eternal Life."

"Eternal Life is the nature of God."

"Then I have now the nature of God?"

"2 Peter 1:4 tells us 'Whereby He hath granted unto us His precious and exceeding great promises; that through these ye may become partakers of the divine nature, having escaped from the corruption that is in the world by lust.' That corruption is spiritual death. You have escaped it by receiving the divine nature, Eternal Life."

"This is wonderful, but I have heard you speak so many times about Righteousness, the ability to stand in God's presence without the sense of guilt or inferiority. When does one get that?"

"Romans 3:26, 'For the showing, I say, of His Righteousness at this present season: that He might Himself be Righteous and the Righteousness of him that hath faith in Jesus.' Have you faith in Jesus as your Savior?"

"I have."

"What does God say that He is to you?"

"He says that He is my Righteousness. I never dreamed I could get anything like that. God Himself has become my Righteousness."

"Yes, did you ever notice 2 Cor. 5:21? 'Him who knew no sin God made to become sin, that we might become the Righteousness of God in Him.' "

"I don't understand that."

"You know that God made Jesus sin with your sin, don't you?"

"But that is awful, that Jesus should be made sin with my sin."

"He did this that you might become the Righteousness of God in Him. If He became sin and you accept Him as your Savior, then you become the Righteousness of God in Him."

"Isn't this wonderful? Has it all been given to me freely?"

"Eph. 2:8-10, 'For by grace have ye been saved through faith; and that not of yourselves, it is the gift of God: not of works, that no man should glory. For we are His workmanship, created in Christ Jesus for good works.' "

"I never dreamed that it could be as easy as that. He says I have been saved by grace on the ground of faith, and that not of myself. This salvation is the gift of God. I did not have to do anything for it. I have been created in Christ Jesus. I am a New Creation. I am a child of God, and it has all come to me as a gift. How I praise Him! How I thank Him through Jesus, my new, wonderful Lord!"

WHAT ARE YOU GOING TO DO ABOUT IT?

You have read this amazing message. What does it mean to you? What will be the aftermath?

You have been let into the heart secrets of the Father. You have seen the death agonies of the Son for you. It has been a personal affair, and you have been saying, "He died for me. He suffered for me. He fought that great battle before He arose from the dead for me.

" 'It was my fight. He conquered Satan for me. It is as though I had fought that battle, suffered all the agonies of it, and conquered the enemy alone. The enemy must forever be a conquered foe. He may be persistent. He may challenge me again and again, but I know I am his master.

" 'I know that in the Name of Jesus I can conquer demons and any affliction that they may bring upon the bodies and minds of men. I am, in that Name, God's instrument of healing and deliverance.' "

You have seen the reality of the New Creation, what it means to have Eternal Life, the nature of God.

You have seen that this New Creation heads up in Jesus; and when He said "I am the vine; ye are the branches," He was uttering a statement of the absolute truth of your union with Him.

You have His life and nature in you. He took your spiritual death and your old nature on the cross and He gives you His life and nature in His Resurrection.

You know that it is possible for you to let this Life dominate your spirit until it gains the ascendency over your reasoning faculties, until really you have the mind of Christ.

You know that His Eternal Life coming into your spirit gives you a creative ability, that you belong to His class now.

Your faith becomes a dominating power, a creative energy.

His Life has become your life, your light, your wisdom, and your ability.

When He told the disciples to tarry in Jerusalem until they received power from on high, that meant that they were to receive God's ability from on High.

You have that ability in you now. It is the nature of God. You are going to let that nature loose.

You are going to learn the secret of freeing the ability of God in you.

You have not only a perfect New Creation, a perfect Redemption wrought by Him, but you have received from Him through this New Creation, His Righteousness.

Righteousness, you know, means the ability to stand in the Father's presence without the sense of guilt, weakness, or inferiority.

Isn't it a strange fact that we need Righteousness to stand in the presence of Satan, and of his works, in the presence of cancers and Tuberculosis with fearless faith?

Nothing will reveal man's utter helplessness and inability and force back upon his consciousness his inferiority like a body filled with cancer.

Yet this Righteousness that is imparted to us at the New Birth gives us a holy boldness in the presence of the works of the adversary.

We are his absolute masters and we know it.

Jesus said, "In my name ye shall cast out demons."

That means mastery over the adversary. This newly discovered Righteousness in Christ gives us courage to use the Name of Jesus in setting men and women free from disease and financial bondage, yes, and every other Satanic control.

It gives a fearlessness in the face of overwhelming circumstances that ordinarily would drive us into defeat.

We have become masters where we served as slaves. We have become freemen where we were held in bondage.

We have become leaders where we did not have courage even to be led.

We have become the light-bearers. We recognize what He said, "Ye are the light of the world."

The Son has set us free. We know what it means to stand in the presence of impossibilities as conquerors.

We are not afraid to walk the sea with the Master. We are not afraid to face the "old serpent" in open combat to set men and women free.

We know we have the Sword of the Spirit that gives us absolute mastery.

We have seen the power and authority of the Word in human lips. The Word is a dead thing in the Bible, but it becomes impregnated with God Himself in the lips of faith.

When we dare say "In Jesus' Name, you are conquered. My Father laid that cancer upon Jesus, and He bore it away, and by His stripes healing belongs to this suffering one," — the Word is as fresh in our lips as it was when Jesus gave it to the apostles.

The Word is a part of God Himself, just as our word is a part of us.

Creation came into being when faith said, "Let there be." That creative element is in that Word today.

"The Words that I speak unto you, they are spirit and they are life."

That means they are creative, they dominate, they bring into being whatever the will of the speaker demands.

How big Christianity becomes. It makes super-men out of slaves.

God takes the "nobodies" and makes "somebodies."

But greater than any of these is the reality of our fellowship with the Father. Fellowship means sharing together. As husband and wife enter into the fellowship of marriage, to share with each other, so we who have been born into the family become fellowsharers with Jesus and the Father.

The Holy Spirit is the One who enables us.

We have His ability, for He promised that when He came He would empower or give ability to the New Creation. We have that ability. We share with Him.

Our fellowship is the light and joy of this wonderful life.

We are walking in the light. There is no darkness in our spirit. Everything that was displeasing to Him has been put out of our life.

We are no longer consecrating, surrendering, and yielding; that belonged to the babyhood state of this marvelous life.

We have grown up into the full stature of the measure of the sons and daughters of God. We are getting under His burdens, we are carrying His loads.

We who are strong, are bearing the burdens of the weak. We are healing them with our faith. We have become the healers, the reconcilers, the helpers in the body of Christ.

We are taking Jesus' place. We have taken over His work. We hear Him say, "Greater things than these shall ye do because I go unto my Father."

We have a right to His Name, His wisdom, His Word, and all His ability. All He is in Himself, He is to us.

The Father gave Him to us. "God so loved the world that He gave His only begotten Son."

He has never taken the gift back. As our Lord, He is our care-taker, our preserver, the mainstay of our life.

"Greater is He that is in you than he that is in the world." We have become God-inside minded.

We remember the day He came into our life. He became our absolute, indwelling Lord.

We know what it means that He is greater than Satan.

He is the One who raised Jesus from the dead. He is the One who made the dead body of Jesus just as sweet and fresh as Heaven's fragrance. He is the One who touched the dead, decaying body of Lazarus and filled it with life and vigor and health.

He is the Renewer, the Healer, and the Sustainer of the church.

He has come into our life. He is to guide us into all reality.

He is to take the things of the Father and the things of Jesus and unveil them to us.

This book we have read is the product of His going into the treasure house and bringing out the long-lost riches of Christ, and turning them over to us.

He is asking us today what we are going to do with them. Are we going to hide them in a napkin, or are we going to invest them?

It is our privilege and our responsibility.

CONCLUSION

You cannot read a book like this without becoming responsible for a new knowledge that has come to you. You must tell others about it.

You should buy as many books as possible and start a circulating library. Lend them to men and women who can appreciate them.

Build up a group of men and women in your community who will dare to act on the Word.

This is a crisis in the history of this country and of civilization. The foundations are being challenged by Satanic power.

FORM A REALITY CLUB

This book, if understood, would revolutionize the church.

It is your business to help make it known.

Get a group to come into your home and read the book to them, explaining it until their hearts are thrilled as yours has been.

Write to us. Take our correspondence course which is a study of the Old and New Testaments in the light of our Redemption in Christ.

Send for our paper "Herald of Life." Read our other books; they are as thrilling as this.

Learn the secret of taking Jesus' place today.

Inspiring Books
by E. W. KENYON

THE BIBLE IN THE LIGHT
OF OUR REDEMPTION
   A Basic Bible Course

ADVANCED BIBLE COURSE
   Studies in the Deeper Life

THE HIDDEN MAN OF THE HEART

WHAT HAPPENED
   From the Cross to the Throne

NEW CREATIONS REALITIES

IN HIS PRESENCE
   The Secret of Prayer

THE TWO KINDS OF LIFE

THE FATHER AND HIS FAMILY
   The Story of Man's Redemption

THE WONDERFUL NAME OF JESUS
   Our Rights and Privileges in Prayer

JESUS THE HEALER
   Has Brought Healing to Thousands

KENYON'S LIVING POEMS

THE NEW KIND OF LOVE

THE TWO KINDS OF FAITH

THE TWO KINDS OF RIGHTEOUSNESS

THE BLOOD COVENANT

THE TWO KINDS OF KNOWLEDGE

SIGN POSTS ON THE ROAD TO SUCCESS

IDENTIFICATION

Order From:
KENYON'S GOSPEL PUBLISHING SOCIETY
P.O. Box 973, Lynnwood, Washington 98046